GREEN MASS

Green Mass

*The Ecological Theology of
St. Hildegard of Bingen*

MICHAEL MARDER

STANFORD UNIVERSITY PRESS
Stanford, California

STANFORD UNIVERSITY PRESS
Stanford, California

Printed in the United States of America on acid-free, archival-quality paper

Library of Congress Cataloging-in-Publication Data

Names: Marder, Michael, 1980– author. | Schuback, Marcia Sá Cavalcante, writer of foreword. | Schuback, Peter, 1947– composer.

Title: Green mass : the ecological theology of St. Hildegard of Bingen / Michael Marder.

Description: Stanford, California : Stanford University Press, 2021. | Includes bibliographical references and index.

Identifiers: LCCN 2021000146 (print) | LCCN 2021000147 (ebook) | ISBN 9781503628847 (cloth) | ISBN 9781503629264 (paperback) | ISBN 9781503629271 (ebook)

Subjects: LCSH: Hildegard, Saint, 1098–1179. | Ecotheology.

Classification: LCC BX4700.H5 M37 2021 (print) | LCC BX4700.H5 (ebook) | DDC 261.8/8—dc23

LC record available at https://lccn.loc.gov/2021000146

LC ebook record available at https://lccn.loc.gov/2021000147

Cover design: Kevin Barrett Kane

Cover illustration: "Plantae Asiaticae rariores," volume 1 (1830), plate 3

Text design: Kevin Barrett Kane

Typeset at Stanford University Press in 10/14 ITC Galliard Pro

CONTENTS

Phytophonies

Echoes of Hildegard of Bingen Today

I

"Listen for once to freshness!" How strange do these words sound today, when nature, life, and the earth itself seem to be on course to deteriorate and disappear? When humans and nonhumans, from animals to inanimate stones, seem to be facing the most lethal threat ever—a threat in comparison to which the apocalyptic tones of the past sound like mild tunes, since the violence of this destruction promises a devastation even more damaging than physical carnage? Where and how might freshness still sound in the world of today, with its planetary politics of fascism and injustice, of misery and distress, of indifference and mistrust? Is there any freshness possible when everything seems to have been already seen, said, and heard? When *the all* of things seems to have been usurped, invaded, and confiscated by the laws of destruction and the spirit of vengeance? Freshness—in which sense? Is it not merely an image, a metaphor? Or is it simply the vestige of an old fresco? Or an ancient word for a desired purity, an expected redemption? Moreover, how should one listen to freshness? How would freshness be audible?

These strange words—with which we ask that freshness be listened to—invite us not only to a series of reflections but also to an

immersive experience. Listen to listening: maybe this is the freshness that remains, as a task to accomplish in our disjointed times.
To listen to listening is, however, only possible when the difference
between the listener and the listened-to is somehow overcome.
Thus, what emerges in the listening experience is the one within
the other, the other within the one. It is the monochordic experience of a sound.

Indeed, a sound is a sound within a sound within another
sound: one in the other, which is itself another, and so forth.
Sound is mysterious insofar as there is no "one" sound—or, better,
insofar as our limited ears listen as though it were one sound rather
than a series of sounds in itself differentiating and differentiated.

The discovery of a tremendous enigma of the one being within
itself, multiple and diverse, of a sound with the whisper of the one
within the other: this discovery is music. We could even call it the
pythagoricity of music, alluding to Pythagoras's discovery of the
monochord or sonometer. But why should it be freshness? In which
sense should music, this one word that already evokes the nine
Muses, be connected to freshness? If every musical experience is
that of infusing the one with the multiple and the diverse, if every
musician and composer performs and embodies this experience,
the sense of freshness within this musical reality must be associated
with a singular woman in Western cultural history: Hildegard of
Bingen, the Benedictine abbess who lived in medieval Germany
between the years 1098 and 1179. Hildegard, the visionary saint
of the life of life, *vita vitae,* as the music of freshness.

II

Hildegard of Bingen was already a legend in her lifetime. She en-
tered the Benedictine order as a child, inspired by the visions she
would continue to have for the rest of her life. She founded mon-
asteries for her nuns; wrote three great volumes of original and
visionary theology (*Scivias* [Know the Ways], *Liber vitae merito-
rum* [Book of the Rewards of Life], and *Liber divinorum operum*

[Book of Divine Works]); and wrote liturgical songs, poems, and the oldest known morality play, titled *Ordo virtutum* (*Order of the Virtues*). She is considered one of the founders of natural history with her two volumes on medicine and cures, the *Physica* and the *Causae et curae*, and was one of the most creative early composers of monophonic music. Besides an extensive correspondence with popes, statesmen, emperors, and other notable figures, she also invented a constructed language, or *lingua ignota*, and would be made a doctor of the church in the twenty-first century. She was a mystical theologian, a healer, an artist, a philosopher, a scientist, and a political voice who in every aspect of her multiple areas of knowledge and intuition drew from the music of freshness—a freshness that, far from any metaphoric meaning, she conceived of as *viriditas,* as greenness, plantness, vegetality.

What is the lesson of Hildegard's vision of the life of life as greening greenness, as *viriditas?* Although used before by Augustine, Gregory the Great, and Hildegard's contemporary, the French nun Heloise, the Latin word *viriditas* gained a unique ontological and metaphysical resonance in Hildegard's writings. There it expresses another sense of *veritas,* of truth, than the common one equating reason and existence, the spirit and the body, the realm of the creator and that of the created. Rather than seeing a correspondence between two orders, realms, or faculties, Hildegard proposes to look at the mystery of plantness, of greening greenness, of growth, advancing what many centuries later another German, the poet Johann Wolfgang von Goethe, thought about in his inquiries on the *Metamorphosis of Plants.* In question here is not how one realm equates or corresponds to the other, but how one grows in and into the other, how one greens forth as the other, the *viriditas*—freshness or greenness—of the othering of life, of the one differentiating in itself, of the music of life. If Hildegard had known ancient Greek, she might have adopted our own invented word, *phytophonia* (from *phyto,* "plant," and *phono,* "sound"), to say in one breath the sound of plantness.

Hildegard's lessons on *viriditas* as music, on phytophonia, in the sense of the one growing into otherness—that is, in the sense of creation—is the subject of this unique book, authored by Michael Marder and musicalized by Peter Schuback. It is a work that meditates in words and sounds on the meaning of *viriditas* as phytophonia, opening ways of knowing today how one is in itself becoming other and of following the paths of creation in a world pierced by *ariditas*, a growing desertification. Even without quoting explicitly the words of Friedrich Nietzsche, another visionary, that "*Die Wüste wächst: weh dem, der Wüsten birgt*" ("The desert grows: woe to him in whom deserts hide"), *Green Mass* listens carefully to the deserts. It listens to the *growth* of the desert beyond boundaries within the capitalist desert, paying attention to how a vagabond little flower grows within and despite the reinforced concrete that today arms the world against the life within itself.

Michael Marder's philosophical work over the last years has been dedicated to thinking about and on the most neglected experience in philosophy, that of plant life and plant-thinking; his is an approach to vegetal being and the mystery of elemental growing. The place of a book on Hildegard's visions of the greening greenness in his philosophy is, of course, more than clear. What is remarkable about Marder's readings of Hildegard's visions of freshness, however, is the attention he pays to how *viriditas* is also the way thoughts grow. Indeed, thoughts are thought not about or on questions, subjects, realities, or experiences, but as plants of life. With Hildegard, Marder learns both how thoughts are the growing branches of life and how this growth is music—hence, that which should be listened to.

III

Green Mass, both the text in your hands and the musical composition that accompanies it, opens with a Prelude and is divided into Verges, Analogies, Resonances, Missives, Ardencies, Anarchies, Kisses, and a Postlude. As a sound is in itself a series of simultaneous sounds, these different chapters or movements should be read and listened to as moments of attention to the different instances of the simultaneous, the mysterious way of the one that grows into its own othering, sounds in words, words in music. Any attempt to find an equation or correspondence between the writing and the music would be fruitless: both grow from a listening *to viriditas*, to greening greenness, and not really to each other. Therefore, one can grow into the other.

The book and the music can be read and heard as phytophonies within phytophonies, as the sounding of greenness within the sounding of greenness, as listening within a listening, wherein the life of life, *vita vitae,* is sensed as the way "the fire of the Spirit gives life to forms and is saint," as Hildegard wrote in one of her poems. My insistence on these repetitive expressions is not a rhetorical procedure. It is instead the way the freshness of listening can be listened to—as echoing, as the growing of each one into the open air of another. If Hildegard wrote poems of poems, songs of songs, and thoughts of thoughts, it was not at all for the sake of turning the soul away from the body of the world, alienating action from theory, imprisoning life in the tower of lifelessness. Much to the contrary, the question was how *viriditas* greens, echoing the one in the other and the other in another. It is, for us today, the demand for thought that keeps an ear close to the earthy ground and lets thinking words be spoken from this listening—decisive words that flourish in the mouth from the abyss of the earth, as flowers grow and plants green on the skin of life.

At a moment when the world seems to be succumbing to despair, when all forms of life are threatened, when not only the annihilation of living beings is legitimated but also the attempt to eradicate being itself, an invitation to "listen for once to freshness" appears as a way out. It pays attention to the incomprehensible dynamics that can take place in not moving, in remaining where one is, spreading multiple branches in the air and deepening multiformed rhizomes under the earth. If it seems difficult to find an answer to the question of where and how we should move today, maybe the answer is one of not trying to give an answer. Perhaps we should stay within the mystery of greening greenness, of *viriditas*, learning to listen to its *lingua ignota*, the unknown score of its sounding, its *phytophonies*.

Marcia Sá Cavalcante Schuback
Södertörn University

NOTE ON SCORES

Recordings are available for listening and download at the Stanford University Press website.

The present scores are not to be taken as written guides for a new performance of the recorded movements. The process of composing electroacoustic music or music to be recorded differs from traditional instrumental composing. Instead, these scores are to be viewed as pictures of my memories of realizing my ideas for the pieces at the very moment when they were composed. As there were many different notes on several sheets of paper, I have tried to make the different characters uniform across all movements. Not everything will be understandable, since these scores were meant for my own purposes. Some things differ from the final performance, and there are some details that not even I can understand myself. A sign in one movement does not mean the same in another, although there is a connection. It is intuition that always has shown me the way, in both music and life.

Peter Schuback

PRELUDE

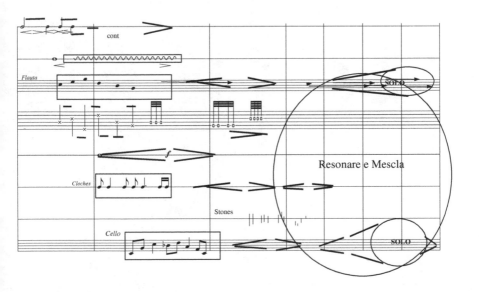

After an introduction, where time is on the move, the actual
Prelude will begin. In itself, the Prelude is also an introductory
set, where it is announced what will happen in the upcoming
movements in the mass. This is an invitation to a space,
which is to be a gathering and a gathered listening.

7 mins 58 secs

Prelude

THIS BOOK BEGAN with a text I wrote at Jason Mohaghegh's invitation in 2017 to contribute to a special issue of *Journal of Comparative and Continental Philosophy*, titled "Soundproof Room." As part of the invitation, Mohaghegh noted: "The only constraint methodologically is that there should be no citations, jargon, or referentiality beyond the encounter with this selected author (i.e. no names or quotes derived from anyone outside the immediate exchange). Rather, the entire production of ideas generated therein should emerge from whatever unique constellation of passages you choose to extract in order to stage the 'soundproof room' experience. The endeavor here is neither a pure scholarly analysis nor historical contextualization but rather a crossing of paths between your own critical imagination and that of another in time."* The author I selected was Hildegard of Bingen, and the resulting article turned out to be an early version of chapter 1 in a larger manuscript.

Very quickly, however, the soundproof room—which I have converted into a resonance chamber for contemporary and premodern concerns, for ecology and theology, philosophy and

* Personal correspondence.

3

mysticism, plant and human wisdom—has come to be a spacious soundproof house. My engagement with Hildegard's writings and especially with her notion of *viriditas* (literally, "the greening green"; figuratively, a self-refreshing vegetal power of creation ingrained in all finite beings) has given an impetus to *Green Mass*, which seeks whatever still remains of vitality in the creases of life's material and spiritual dimensions, contemplative and engaged attitudes, visual and auditory registers.

The title *Green Mass* is charged with a double meaning. It refers, at the same time, to the way plants have been assessed as the heaviest biomass by far among all forms of life on earth and to a musical composition in Christian liturgy that is "colored" on the model of George Gershwin's *Rhapsody in Blue*. The mixing of the crudely material (weight, heaviness) and the refined, spiritual (church music) connotations of this noun in English is no accident. It is my contention that Hildegard has no equal in drawing a higher sense from the most mundane physical realities, that is to say, in teasing out a theology from an ecology and, vice versa, in endowing theology with an ecological meaning.

I do not, for all that, intend to reconstruct something like a system of Hildegard's ecological theology. Instead, I occupy myself with the most emblematic sites where spirituality and materiality intermingle, from fire ("Ardencies") to divine and finite existences, lacking, for different reasons and with distinct effects, beginnings and ends ("Anarchies"). I argue, in fact, that to systematize Hildegard's writings is to betray them, to make them crystallize into quasi-mineral formations, while turning a blind eye to the vegetal metamorphoses that operate at the levels of these writings' content and form.

Each chapter, then, revolves around a theme (also understood in the musical sense) in her ecological theology, with careful attention paid to the expressions, tropes, and allusions in Hildegard's Latin. In and of themselves, my translations of the relevant parts of her corpus (including, among others, *Physica, Scivias,* the epistles,

Liber divinorum operum, and *Solutiones triginta octo quaestionum),*
and the hymns gathered in *Symphonia,* may be of value to those
reading the book in English, as extant translations are scarce and,
when available, abridged, not at all faithful to the original, or both.
But the guiding thread of the book is *viriditas,* itself a synecdoche
for vegetal life, which bridges the worlds of spirit and matter and,
ultimately, theology and ecology.

To confess, I feel particular affinity to Hildegard, in that I
see her vegetalizing theology in much the same way as I've attempted to vegetalize the Western philosophical canon. Such
efforts cannot help but lead to a delicious perversion: divine and
metaphysical realities that are supposed to be immutable start
growing, metamorphosing, and, yes, decaying when grazed by
leaves and flowers, roots and branches. It is in this context that I
focus on "Analogies" and "Resonances" that are among the de-
vices Hildegard avails herself of as she struggles to reveal the fluid
similitudes and symphonic connections between psychic states
and faculties, plant organs and phenomena, religious figures and
biological processes.

I am also aware, of course, that the liturgical sense of "mass,"
announced in the title of the book and hinting at Hildegard's ideas
on the symphonicity of being as well as her musical theory and
practice, cannot be dealt with by textual means alone. That is why
this project is not only mine; it is a collaboration with Swedish cellist
and composer Peter Schuback. Thanks to Peter's work *Hildegard
Mass,* the resonances of ecology and theology are awash in the reverberations of music and philosophy, thinking and singing being.

So, the soundproof house that is this book is anything but.
In place of walls, readers will find here vibrating membranes, not
resistant to but facilitating the passage of sound—in short, what
I have just called a *resonance chamber.* How does the dwelling at
the heart of ecology fit this description? Is "resonance chamber"
another way of saying "ecology"? Come to think of it, hasn't ecology always conjugated an abode (*oikos*) with a certain sonority of

logos, which names, among other things, a discourse, speech, a spoken word. *Oikologia* is where reverberating voices abide. One of Hildegard's many achievements is to have indirectly shaped this rare sense of ecology.

⚭

It would seem at first glance that the insights of *Green Mass* are somewhat anachronistic. What can we learn about the current environmental crisis from texts by a twelfth-century Benedictine abbess? And why combine ecology with theology at all?

The answer to the second question actually holds a clue to the first. Theology and ecology are codes for mental-psychic-spiritual and material-extended-embodied relations, respectively. Their articulation in vitality, by means of *viriditas,* has the potential to heal the split—which was exacerbated by Descartes, whose philosophy it predates—responsible for putting the planet on the brink of an environmental disaster. The onto-theological metaphysical tradition, already palpable in Pauline Christianity, in the works of the gnostics, and in Neoplatonism, has treated existence here below as infinitely less valuable and stable than the true reality of spirit. As a result, the destruction of this world, which, from a metaphysical standpoint, is mere fog or a veil before our eyes, is viewed as nothing terrible; on the contrary, the world's coming to an end is supposed to celebrate the final victory of truth and virtue over falsehood and sin. It is as a consequence of secularizing this logic and its economic ramifications that the planet has been transformed into a dump for the industrial activities of Western societies. The ecological nightmare we are living (or dying) in today is a hardly disguised cumulative outcome of the ideas and practices that have molded Western theological tradition for millennia.

Though embedded within that tradition, Hildegard articulates ecology and theology otherwise in an endeavor that is not at all outdated, insofar as it occupies itself with the roots of today's environmental disaster. As she imbues ecological relations with theological meaning and suffuses theology with ecological—largely vegetal—connotations, Hildegard intimates that the abuse of the earth and its issue, of the sky, water, animals, and even minerals, is not qualitatively different from the ill treatment of everything and everyone that is holy in Judeo-Christianity. The associations she foregrounds go beyond Augustine's allegorical symbolism: physics and physiology *express* the truth of spirit, while something of spirit is *manifest* in the most mundane phenomena. Ever a physician, she proposes an eco-theological cure to the eco-theological disorder that is the rift between matter and spirit.

Crucially, for Hildegard, the drama of sin and salvation is played out between the environmental poles of the forest and the desert, the revitalizing power of *viriditas* and the deadly force of *ariditas,* the latter's dry, scorching heat eerily anticipating anthropogenic global warming and the threat of mass extinction due to catastrophic climate change. On the one hand, the contrast between eternal and ephemeral being softens under the influence of *viriditas* that inflects finite life with a potentially infinite thrust of self-regeneration. On the other, *ariditas* hardens the divides between the body and the soul, matter and spirit, the ensouled body and its environment. It deprives life of the conditions necessary for living on, separates the living from life, exhausts life itself. Described in this fashion, *ariditas* is indistinguishable from metaphysics and traditional theology.

As for our own, presumably postmetaphysical, age, Hildegard portrays it perfectly in chapter 46 of the fifth vision included in book 2 of *Scivias.* Here, God decries unbridled human mastery and control over creation: "I had a green field in my power [*Viridem agrum in potestate mea habui*]. Did I give it to you, O human, so that you would make it put forth whatever fruit you wished?" (*Scivias* II.5.46; CCCM 43, 214). The greenness of the field discussed on these pages is outer and inner, that of plants and of the heart of an oblate "dedicated and sanctified to me in baptism." Having dared rashly touch (*temere tangere*) not so much the green field itself as that which makes it green, having meddled with the power (*potestas*) that is not theirs, human beings produce a strange effect (*effectus*) "that is neither dry nor fresh" and "a world that is neither dead nor alive [*Unde nec aridus nec viridis effectus est, ita quod nec saeculo mortuus est nec saeculo vivit*]" (*Scivias* II.5.46; CCCM 43, 214–15). Just as an oblate dies to the world while continuing to live in it, so, *mutatis mutandis,* our world dies to us, who continue trying to inhabit it and to keep harvesting its late fruit.

Today's predominant growth—the desert's self-reproduction on an expanding scale, both inside and outside us—matches Hildegard's vision. But it is not only the earth that is becoming a desert; the world, too, is desertified, the realms of matter and spirit converging on their mutual devastation. What does the end of the world look like for a world that, neither dead nor alive, is in itself, in its very modus operandi, a scurrying to the end of itself and of the earth? Can we, still or already, espy ourselves across centuries, ways of thinking, and languages in a visionary portrait Hildegard has painted?

VERGES

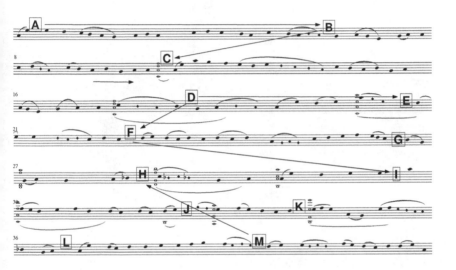

A still worshipping, innocent recitative about the future and
memories. The movement consists of several choices about
branching roads and where they lead. It is an expectation
of the coming and an innocent farewell to the past.

4 mins 17 secs

Verges

LISTEN FOR ONCE TO FRESHNESS! Hildegard's voice is still fresh—ever-fresh, ever-green—despite having sounded over eight hundred years ago. What resonates in it is nothing like the force of the monumental "classics" that, regardless of shifting historical contexts and circumstances, are supposed to stay eternally relevant in their immovable veracity. Her figure is not that of a towering rock that overshadows the subsequent history of thought, let alone the tenebrous archeology of the unthought and the unthinkable but intensely and mystically experienced. It is, rather, that of a tree, of plantness or vegetality, of greenness and greening (*viriditas*), perpetually on the verge of renewal, of rejuvenation, reaffirming a promise instilled in creation.

With a garden in her name and cosmic vegetality in her visions, Hildegard intuited the sonorous sorority of being poetically, linguistically, conceptually, and musically expressed in her symphony in green. The secret to her voice's freshness is that its tonalities and modulations echo vegetal vitality, which, ostensibly mute, furnishes a language for singing the world as a whole. Her story is an example of what happens when one indelibly ties one's own fate to the destiny of plants that cover the earth and englobe the entire region of a burgeoning, growing self-emergence the Greeks called *phusis.*

We are still on the verge of the opening chapter, which is the book's verge of sorts. Would it be wise to ask at this point what was in the beginning, on a unique verge thought to be incipient, as Hildegard sees or hears it?

In principio omnes creature viruerunt, / in medio flores floru-erunt; / postea viriditas descendit. "In the beginning, all creation was verdant, / in the middle, flowers blossomed; / later, *viriditas* came down" (*Ordo* Epil. 343–45; CCCM 226, p. 521). This narrative diverges somewhat from the biblical story, according to which the newly created earth was barren, devoid of life. Hildegard indicates that "all creation," including the terrestrial fold prior to the emergence of plants, is a site of the greening green. The virginal verge, from which existence commences in the absence of an absolute principle (the one and only true genesis), is verdant. Conceivably, flowers blossomed in the middle of a green beginning; however, the progression of the lines from the epilogue of Hilde-gard's *Ordo virtutum* (*Order of the Virtues*) suggests otherwise. Just as angiosperms are latecomers on the evolutionary scene, so flowers announce a departure from the universal greenness and greening of the beginning within the framework of ecological theology. Their vibrantly multicolored petals enchant and detract from that which is a color and not a color, from *viriditas* saturating the flora and the formally nonvegetal realms alike.

Flowers are, furthermore, a kind of centerpiece, placed in the middle of the natural-spiritual history Hildegard is writing. Slotted between the plenitude of the verdant beginning and the retreat of *viriditas* auguring de-creation, they are at once the mediators and a midpoint on a downward slope ending with *ariditas,* the advance of dryness that poses a grave threat to the greening green-ness of life. With the flowers foreshadowing fruits, the Fall and the fall (the human betrayal of *viriditas* and its fatal diminution) are drawing nigh.

Could Hildegard have foreseen the devastating desertification of the earth attributable to deforestation and global warming? Are these the palpable effects of the intangible retreat of *viriditas*? Whatever the answer to these speculations first voiced in the Prelude, in *Order of the Virtues* there is nothing inevitable about the history of life as a Fall, etched onto our minds along with a certain conception of energic systems necessarily tending to entropy. We ought to "remember this: that the fullness which was created in the beginning / need not have run dry [*memor esto, quod plenitudo que in primo facta est / arescere non debuit*]" (*Ordo* Epil. 351–52; CCCM 226, p. 521). The idea of entropy gives us a false image of energy and of the universe. The Latin verb *descendere*, which I have translated as "to come down," attached to *viriditas* at a late stage relative to the beginning, means both a decrease of its refreshing power and the descent of *viriditas* embodied in the figure of Christ, who arrives, precisely, to renew this natural-spiritual capacity for renewal. The beginning recommences, time and again, anarchically, from the vegetal verge that, finite yet resilient, pushes against a spreading dryness. It is not—or, at least, it need not be—depleted in the end, in the final exhaustion of what was once bountiful.

In the beginning was spring. It began without anything verging on it and without it verging on anything: no winter behind, no summer ahead. In itself, it was a verge for the greenness of existence, for existence as a greening forth. That is the initial *viriditas* Hildegard invokes, very much in keeping with Virgil and his view of spring in *The Georgics*, as well as with her contemporary William of Conches, who in his *Dragmaticon* identifies spring with the season of creation. It is also the condition of Adam and Eve, who lived as though they were a pair of precious hothouse plants in the Garden of Eden. Their Fall is tied not to the luxuriant green of vegetation nor to flowers but to fruits, corresponding to the moment of *viriditas* "coming down" (*viriditas descendit*). The fate of the fruit is to fall to the ground in the state of ripeness; eating from the forbidden variety that grows on the Tree of Knowledge of Good and Evil triggers the Fall of an unripe humanity. By that time, which is the beginning of secular time and of world history (another verge!), the spring is over, the paradisiac plenitude of *viriditas* having drawn to a close. *Ariditas* is now the order of the day. But what prevents *viriditas* from running dry entirely? And how is it possible for *viriditas* to gain strength the further away it is from the beginning?

The answer may lie in a juxtaposition of the first spring and the regenerative verge it has become in the seasonal cycle. As we know it, spring is a beginning that begins after the end, when the dead of winter has ebbed away. Despite coming on the heels of the end, its fullness is not that of a completed actuality. Spring is pregnant with the future, with what is not yet, what is on the verge of being, the promise of a new beginning. It announces the resurrection of nature and the replenishment of *viriditas*. After the Fall, spring is the impersonal prototype of Jesus, who, in the footsteps of older Mesopotamic and North African traditions, reanimates the energy-matter of creation on the cross, with the wood of the cross—it, too, admitted into sublime vegetal afterlife upon the cutting of the tree it was made of. His mother (*mater, materia*) is in close semantic and ontological proximity to spiritual matter rooted in the world of plants. "You are that luminous matter [*es tu illa lucida materia*]," Hildegard exclaims in her "Antiphon for the Virgin" (*Symph.* 10.12) where she also refers to Mary as *prima materia* (10.15), the "prime matter" or the "primary matrix" of redemption, the verge of another spring.

The descending portion of the orbit, in which *viriditas* rotates, acquires a double meaning. It describes, on the one hand, the sapping of vegetal freshness, the drying up, already in Adam's and Eve's lifetimes, of the self-renewing power that pervades creation, the power of finite existence to reinvent and restore itself. On the

other hand, it reflects the earthward movement of *viriditas* in a
divine incarnation that counters and reverses the steady advance of
ariditas. The ambiguity of greenness "coming down" is unavoidable: the concentration of *viriditas* in Mary and Jesus repeats *and*
undoes the drop that the Fall represents.

Hildegard will, nonetheless, refuse to identify Mary with a ripe
fruit holding the seed of salvation. Prior to fruits and flowers, she
greens. She is "the greenest branch [*viridissima virga*]" (*Symph.*
19.1), on which the flower of redemption will blossom: "the time
has come for you to blossom in your branches [*venit tempus quod
tu floruisti in ramis tuis*]" (19.2). We will return to this verge of
the verge, to the virgin (*virgo*) who is a *virga*, with the view to
unsnarling its (and her) multiple implications, complications, and
co-implications. Suffice it to note for now that, while a fruit falls
down and leads to the downfall of humanity, the greenest branch
lifts its leaves and the flower of redemption, hoisting them up. In a
genuinely revolutionary move, in a counterclockwise rotation, time
is rewound from its late fructiferous stage to the middle (flower;
Jesus) and, further back, to the incipient plenitude of *viriditas*
(green branch; Mary). It flows from the fall and the summer to
the spring, a period when the green is on the verge of appearing,
when sprouts develop and buds give way to leaves, those ongoing
iterations of vegetal surfaces exposed to the sun.

Rather than concealment of a seed in the fruit, exposure and
openness define the being of Mary and Jesus. A pregnancy that
is a blossoming, not a coming to fruition, departs from a strict
teleology of accomplishment. A flower may or may not be productive of something else; it may or may not be an evanescent stage
on the predetermined path to the fruit, in consonance with how
the virgin conception and birth of Jesus deviate from the tenets
of reproductive sexuality. In the greenest branch and its flower,
viriditas is not exhausted, as it is, in different senses, in the fruit
and in *ariditas*. Nor does this flower, which at an auspicious time
"blossom[s] in your branches," seductively divert a fascinated gaze

from the green monochrome. The flower is the lucidity of matter, of the mother herself, of the branched matrix. Lucidity hypostatized, one might say.

Insubordinate to externally posited ends, *viriditas* is efficacious beyond any calculations of efficient realization. Having nothing to do with the judgment that an action is performed "for nothing" or "for the sake of something," joy and enjoyment overflow verdant being at its superficies, in the marvelous proliferation of open vegetal surfaces, the leaves and the flowers verging on the other (sunlight, insects . . .). *Viriditas* suspends the end as a point of abrupt termination and as a goal to be accomplished by resorting to this or that means. Neither ending nor unending, it is inexhaustible in a manner totally distinct from the myth of eternal presence. That is why "the fullness [*plenitudo*] which was created in the beginning / need not have run dry": the second spring, kept in reserve as it awaits its hour, scintillates with the vigor of the first that has neither ended nor not-ended. The verge is on the verge. That is also why, thanks to the greenest branch, all that was dry (*arida*) "appears . . . in full green [*apparuerunt . . . in viriditate plena*]" (*Symph.* 19.4): the appearing of what appears so long as it appears, be it a desert, is brimming with *viriditas* on the surfaces that present themselves to sense and to the senses, all the while these surfaces, too, sense and make sense of the world.

Hildegard's Mary is not *gratia plena* (full of grace) but *viriditate plena* (full of greenness and greening), or, better, she is *gratia plena* insofar as she is *viriditate plena*. Her plenitude graciously and gratuitously wells over in the material and maternal form of *viriditas*. This form has little to do with a hollow cask receptive toward any contents whatsoever. Essence is the skin of appearances, the surface with its essentially superficial feature: color. "Full of green" is fundamentally a matter of appearance, inscribed into the quasi-concept of *viriditas*, where *how* something presents itself gains in significance over *what* is presented. A modality of existence prevails over abstract being in this phenomenology of the verge, where *spring* is the name for the time of coming to appearance, the flourishing of and on the surface, and the confluence of greening and greenness.

At the same time, there are no metaphors and allegories in what Hildegard's voice conveys. *Viriditas* is not the vigorous force of plants symbolically transposed onto other forms of life, including divine vitality, any more than the event of resurrection is a figurative interpretation of natural processes—for instance, the reawakening of vegetation after its wintry slumber. To Hildegard's mind, the opposite is true. The rebirth of nature in the spring is a reenactment of the divine spectacle, not the other way around. Winter is a cooling down of the world, more than that of worldly entities and regions, the cooling down that bespeaks a flight of spirit, the world getting out of touch with itself. In "Antiphon for Saint Ursula" winter arrives with "the serpent's breath [*hyems de flatu serpentis*]" (*Symph.* 61.5), its seduction inhibiting the life-giving warmth of creaturely coexistence in time and space.

It is in a rigorously nonallegorical, nonsymbolic sense that we, humans, are plants: together we partake of the greening greenness that is undeniably more obvious and sensuously present in actual vegetation. *Viriditas* is the energy of creation and of re-creation; the green essence it names is to be heard not only as an adjective that describes a real quality of things (i.e., a color) but also as a verb that denotes the active making-green, a greening of the world in the course of its becoming-world. The energy of creation, transmitted through the divine Word to the creatures, is irreducible to a pure potentiality devoid of substantive realization. Whereas plants are visibly and invisibly green, humans retain only a dash of invisible greenness, not as a substantive quality but as an activity of making-green, connected to the creative energy boiling in the Word. That is to say, the incarnation of *viriditas* in us is less perfect than it is in plants, its perceptible (chlorophyllic) facets missing from human existence.

⊷

We are plants *and* we are the others of plants. Can these assertions be equally and simultaneously valid? I should, perhaps,
specify that we are the plants' others who stray from and try to
deplete the energetic fullness we are enjoined to embody and
who, our divagations notwithstanding, remain plants: camou-
flaged, unrecognizable, obscure. *Viriditas* is lopsided and perverted in us, unless a more daring assertion that we *are* the
perversion of *viriditas* is warranted. In addition to a lacuna of
sensuously manifest greenness in human carnality, our enactment
of *viriditas* sets it against itself, contributing to the global spread
of aridity and causing everything fresh to wither, as we interfere with the self-refreshing capacities of life. If the Word of God
is verdant, if God's creative finger is green—"O, the greening
greenness of the finger of God [*O viriditas digiti Dei*]" (*Symph.*
42.1)—then desertification and deforestation uproot the Word
and thwart divine energy. In fact, seeing that *ariditas* is a negative manifestation of *viriditas*, desertification and deforestation
turn this Word and this energy against themselves. Through the
human, the finger of God does battle with itself.

Bereft of visible greenness, humanity also rejects the invisible
greening that binds us to the rest of creaturely life in an insistent
repetition of the creative act by this life itself. In contrast, along its
noninstitutional axis, religion reties the thread of *viriditas* always
on the verge of being cut at a spot where substantive greenness
touches active greening or there where the human creature un-
dercuts itself along with its world. Hildegard does the retying in
her unique style: adding her voice through vegetal mediations to
the Word of God, saying-naming-singing-thinking *viriditas*, from
which she borrows, unable to contain it (or herself, for that matter),
her own freshness. (The word *viriditas* and the thing it names are
uncontainable; they flood—*cum ei viriditatem infundit*, "flooded
with *viriditas*"—the ear and the flesh, like abundant morning dew
that saturates the grass [*Symph.* 17.6]. This same overflow is behind
the *plenum* of sheer joy and enjoyment in the virgin conception.)

Viriditas that verges on being cut is a corollary to the human perversion, to the perversion that is the human, traversed by a colossal energy asymmetry. The time of the verge is discontinuous. Shrouded in tense expectancy, it is when one state is about to end and another shows signs of beginning. Verging on something else entirely, an event is at a point between the end and another beginning. So, a voice on the verge of speaking or singing hovers between silence and sound (for instance, as one draws one's breath), even if silence itself is vibrant, vibrating with the sonority of the verdant Word that precedes and succeeds the utterance. A spatial position on the verge is similarly fragile, lodged at the edge of a narrow surface, shaped (should we seek guidance from etymology) as a twig, a shoot, or a slender green branch. Everything is uncertain, twisting and turning between the point of an event and the edges of a surface, between a noun and a verb (*a* verge and *to* verge: energy's substantive and active-verbal expressions), between the visible and the invisible, the past and the future, the plant and the other plant or plants' other.

The verge is fragile, but fragility is not exempt from the verge's reversals, its tendency to swivel, to pivot on itself, to turn in a spiral around its axis, as in the nutational movement of plant growth, to contradict itself and to thrive on self-contradiction. Though tender, the shoot is strong; against the force of gravity, it shoots up from the earth and carries leaves and flowers skyward. When Hildegard calls Mary "a leafy branch [*frondens virga*]" (*Symph.* 15.1), she is playing on the verge, with the verge shaped as a virgin (*virgo*) and a branch (*virga*). Curiously enough, in her vegetal apparition, Mary is incredibly virile: "standing [*stans*]" in her nobility (15.2); setting free "us, frail ones [*nos debiles*]" (15.5); "raising us up [*erigendum nos*]" (15.9). In a vegetal carnival of sexual difference, the branch is rigid and erect, its behavior prefiguring the male member, the penis, which once bore in Latin the same common name, *virga*.

Later, we will come across other references to the Virgin's virility, according to which she is revealed to be stronger than her son. Typically considered the antipodes of human sexuality, virginity and virility belong to a broad textual and contextual frame uniting them with vegetality, verdancy, vigor, life (*vita*), virtue, and veracity in Hildegard's oeuvre. Not to mention with the verge. One consequence of this lineage for our discussion is glaring: the cut of *viriditas* factored into the human condition after the Fall is the cut of castration. Our alienation from the actual greenness of the plant world and from the greening power of life emasculates us with reference to the masculine and the feminine connotations of *viriditas*, striking at the root *vir* before its branching out into virginity and virility. Ever a healer, Hildegard strives to cure, to rebind, this deep wound that is the original sin (broadly understood as a rebellion against *viriditas*), the wound around which human identity has in the meantime accreted as a thwarting of the freshness of existence. What are the treatments she prescribes?

1. *Cutting the cut.* Assuming that the forbidden fruit is the material cause of the sin, responsible for the castration of humanity, the mission of the Holy Spirit is to cut it loose from the tree: "But you hold a sword ever / ready to cut off [*abscidere*] / what the poisonous apple [*noxiale pomum*] / brings forth through the darkest homicide [*nigerrimum homicidium*]" (*Symph.* 27.5). With nearly surgical precision, resorting to a negation of the negation, Hildegard recommends cutting out that which cuts humans off from the root of life, that which kills the human in "the darkest homicide," whence humanity emerges *qua* humanity. She then proceeds to cut the fruit from the divine-vegetal story she is writing, so that only leaves and flowers endure. We must fall out with the Fall, let it fall by the wayside, retrace our steps and missteps, making a detour (into the past as much as into the future) to greening greenness before it has yielded its late and poisoned fruit. Perversity must be perverted, turned around, bent, inclined toward something or someone else, verging on another state, if hopes for a cure are to bear their nonfruit.

2. *Restitching the lost phallus.* Here is one of the oldest compensatory techniques on the books: a shaft of light becomes a powerful replacement for castrated urges, desires, and even organs. In her "Responsory for Virgins," Hildegard exclaims: "O most noble *viriditas* / that is rooted in the sun [*que radicas in sole*] / . . . You blush like dawn / and burn like a solar flame [*et ardes ut solis flamma*]" (*Symph.* 56.1–2, 56.10–11). Through the virgin, who embodies *viriditas*, the rays of greening green reach every corner of the earth and give off light and heat, the two classical "powers of fire" enlivening portions of creation that have dried up and perished, not least due to the excess of these igneous powers. Parallel to the history of metaphysics and its uneasy relation to vegetal life, divine *viriditas* operates a reversal: it flips the plant, so that the root is not in the ground below but in the sky above—"you take root in the sun" (*radicas in sole*). Rather than being mired in unconscious existence, the root shines and burns, as it does in John, "the sweet chosen one," "who in the most intense ardor / flashed forth as a root [*effulsisti, radix*]" (*Symph.* 36.2–3). Where Hildegard differs from the metaphysical tradition is in her refusal to render vegetality merely symbolic: "taking root in the sun" is "the most noble *viriditas.*" The greening green of plants depends on the life-giving power of the physical sun, not on the metaphysical double of the celestial body. To turn back to vegetality and the solar blaze, to the one through the other (but also, as we will discover in this book, to the one *as* rooted in the other), is to turn down the virtual supplement of ideal light and eternal life.

3. *Discovering plenitude in a perceived lack.* Methodically—if also intuitively, by improvising—Hildegard shifts the center of gravity in power relations so as to address the imbalance within *vir*, between virginity and virility. In the absence of fruits, her efforts actually involve the opposite of gravity: a corporeal elevation of vegetal growth. The branch is a mobile support lifting other plant parts, birds, insects, and small animals, while staying in touch with the terrestrial sphere. Mary hoists Jesus, who carries the weight of

the world on his shoulders. She is *virga mediatrix*, "the mediating branch," for the blossoming of a "beautiful flower" (*Symph.* 18.2, 18.7). Far from a mere receptacle, she (and not only she; John the Baptist does so as well) plays Jesus's part before he himself does. The middle of the middle, a mediator for Christ the Mediator, she is nothing like a faded backdrop for divine self-sacrifice. Despite being "only" a branch, she embodies *viriditas*, the vegetal life that flourishes in the middle between earth and sky, light and darkness, and that is the middle from which the world stems in its ongoing regeneration. On the vegetal verge, a beginning that is not absolute (i.e., not arising *ex nihilo*) is the middle: the phrase "In the beginning, all creation was verdant" says as much, in the same breath saying and unsaying, contra-dicting the beginning. There, plenitude bursts through an appearance of lack, through the fundamentalist and productivist perspectives on the middle as *already not* at the fecund beginning and *not yet* at the fructified end.

Hildegard's third cure is an overarching intervention into the worlds of plants and humans, destabilizing and upending power relations. The subtraction of the vegetal middle—the milieu of growth with its own meaning above and beyond the logic of governing principles and commanding ends—from a polarized field recalls the extraction of a rib from Adam for the purpose of creating Eve. "How great," Hildegard writes, "is / in its power the side of man [*in viribus suis latus viri*] / from which God produced [*produxit*] the form of woman" (*Symph.* 20.4a). The discarded and superfluous element, be it the "excluded middle" of vegetal becoming or a rib Adam could live without, is what bestows sense on the whole that gives it up. Exception is universalized.

Formal logic excludes the middle, forcefully and overtly. It does so in a foundational act tantamount to an admission that it is unable to think life, growth, metamorphosis, movement, which is, at bottom, the admission that it is unable to think, pure and simple. Its practitioners construe what remains after the act of exclusion as an idiosyncratic strength that affords them crystal (mineral, not vegetal) clarity. In a cognate development, older than formal logic, the historical disempowerment of women under patriarchy is a ruse thrown over the surplus of power that they *are*, as opposed to the one they *have*. The highest concentration of the power of man (*viribus . . . viri*), Hildegard observes countering formal logical axioms, is not in man; it lies or swirls on the side of a woman, in the side Adam can no longer claim as his own. The rib is a verge, an ersatz *virga*, stronger than the male member it is reminiscent of. And it is no longer Adam's. Crossing, as she is apt to do, from Adam and Eve to Jesus and Mary, from the rib to the branch and from the forbidden fruit to the sublime flower, Hildegard thus dares sing: "O, the sweetest branch [*suavissima virga*] / . . . what a great power [*magna virtus*] this is!" (*Symph.* 21.1, 21.3).

Eve is not the sole point of reference for Mary's virginal varia-tions on the verge, however. Embracing both sides of sexual differ-ence, the greenest branch that betokens the arrival of humanity's second spring is also negatively comparable to Adam: "Your leaves flourished [*floruisti*] / in another way / than Adam produced / the entire humankind [*omne genus humanum / produceret*]" (*Symph.* 20.1b). Because Mary does not bear fruit, the virginal verge is not productive. Humanity thrives on it otherwise: generated more exuberantly, more faithfully to the greening green of *viriditas*, than a productivist ideology would allow. That ideology is at the heart of the Fall. The way Adam generates the rest of humanity is in accord with the original sin, albeit not in the usual sense of a maculate, stained conception (Eve is conspicuously absent here). He is fascinated with the forbidden fruit, drawn to it at the expense of other plant parts, among them the flowers, judged meaningless in and of themselves, deficient and incomplete as the fruit's mere anticipations or potentially empty promises. So much so that the obsession with fruitful productivity interferes with a flourishing that, in addition to its independent meaning and value, is the necessary precondition for fecundity.

Productivism and the teleology of fruition that informs it severely restrict the range of what may be legitimately engendered, particularly in a human form. Since, divided at the very least into the male and the female, the human is not one, the resulting form, the shape of the human, cannot be a product, static in its identity. The language of productivism nonetheless persists: the tragedy is that, just as God "produced [*produxit*] the form of woman" from the verge that was Adam's rib, so Adam produces (*produceret*) the human genus, bewitched by an exceptional product of the plant kingdom, "the poisoned apple." The exceptionality of the forbidden fruit is that it is precisely a *fruit, produce,* a product of plant life made to serve as a model of successful accomplishment in our conduct in general and in sexual reproduction in particular.

All this makes God culpable not only as the *producer* of human forms and not only as the creator of the Tree of Knowledge but also as the giver of the commandment *Be fruitful and multiply!* that transforms fruit into a verb in the plural imperative (the Hebrew *p'ru*) and mandates the couple's fruition in its progeny. The forbidden fruit is, of course, not the same as any other sort of fruit, nor is it synonymous with fruitfulness. Still, it is not by a sheer coincidence that God's positive command and prohibition both revolve around fruit: their entwinement means that to obey the divine order is to sin, and to sin is to follow God's injunction. Fruits absorb into themselves and neutralize the difference between the *do* and the *don't.* This constitutive perversion does not lend itself to being easily remedied; the bids to reverse it by keeping to a behavior believed to be righteous are futile. *Ergo,* the roundabout formulations of Hildegard's "cures."

❧

A virginal reconfiguration of humanity is meant to steer us away from the logic of achievement, according to which any and every process is overshadowed by, consumed, and consummated in the final product. An alternative energy is at stake on the verge: the fullness of leafing and flowering, the energy of the surface that, rooted in the sun, does not follow an inevitably entropic trajectory and that reinvents accomplishment on the hither side of fruitfulness. The path of *viriditas* is not a means to an end that, once actualized, would erase the tracks that led to it. The greening green is the means *and* the end, the one folded into the other, complicated and coimplicated in engendering (without producing) finite existence.

With vegetal freshness for a linchpin—unless it is a brush for painting the human and the divine green—Hildegard's energy does not derive from an untainted and undying metaphysical source, the conventional monotheistic God. *Viriditas* goes along with the birth and death of God who is the same as and totally other than the deity of monotheism. Colored in with the greening green, the outlines of Mary and Jesus are apparent in the coming to appearance of growth and the decay of plants, beckoning with the afterlife of regeneration from the lowliness of dirt. The virginity of the verge Hildegard celebrates is not the untouched, primordial purity of an ideal; on the contrary, the verge is originally contaminated by that upon which it verges on more than one side, *viriditas* beginning in the middle, the beginning beginning in the middle . . . The greenest branch's fragility and strength, flexibility and carrying capacity, are, therefore, not analogous to the always rigid and thoroughly dried-up erection of the metaphysical edifice left brittle by the retreat of vegetal freshness. The movements of the branch oscillate between an ascent, hoisting the sublime flower of salvation, and a flourishing descent—incarnation, conception—that is other than the fall, or the Fall. Fulfillment abides between and within these contrapuntal movements.

Shorn of omnipotence, the "virginal branch [*virginea virga*]" of Christ's birth (*Symph.* 58.3) delineates a new set of coordinates for energy and power, which turns out to be all the more powerful the more it gives up the illusion of being all-powerful. A revaluation of actuality and potentiality occurs on the verge of another day, "as if at dawn [*quasi aurora*]" (*Symph.* 22.10). From the standpoint of the powers that be, the branch and the flower blossoming on it are powerless: playful, superficial, colorful, "merely" ornamental, childish, forever immature inasmuch as they do not culminate in a fruit. But that is the perspective of the preceding day, which is already over, which is *always* already over, happily at its end before having actually ended. There is no arguing with the partisans of a fruitful dusk, insensitive to verges, to the virginity of time that recommences each year in the spring, each day at dawn, and each moment in a risky leap to the next, also complete in itself. Impenetrable to them is the accomplishment one may procure not in closure and not in the round enclosure of the fruit but in the opening of existence, in unfurling leaves and petals. It is in this vein that I read Hildegard's lines: "Today a closed gate [*clausa porta*] / has opened to us [*aperuit nobis*] / the door that the serpent shut on a woman. / From there, the flower of Virgin Mary / gleams at dawn" (*Symph.* 11.1–5).

The story of Hildegard's "verginal" thought, as I have presented it, is based largely on her *Symphonia*. In other writings, she seems accepting of fruits that, in the tradition of Augustinian exegesis, signify works of faith. For example, her mystical visions collected in *Scivias* contain affirmations of this sort: "The mercy of God's grace, like the sun, will illuminate the person, the breath of the Holy Spirit, like the rain, will water him, and so discernment, like the tempering of the air, will lead him to the perfection of good fruits [*ad perfectionem bonorum fructuum ducet*]" (*Scivias* I.4.25; CCCM 43, p. 84). Even more troubling for our argument are some of the formulations on the subject of virginity as "the most beautiful apple among all the apples of the valley [*pulcherrimum pomum inter omnia poma convallium*]" (*Scivias* I.2.24; CCCM 43, p. 30). (To be fair, Hildegard still omits—cuts?—fruits from the delightful splendor of paradise, "which blooms with the *viriditas* of flowers and grass and the charms of aromatic herbs" [*Scivias* I.2.28; CCCM 43, p. 32].) What is responsible for this sea change in her attitude to fruits?

I see two possible explanations.

First, the poetic form of *Symphonia* with its melodic consonances, such as *virginea virga*, may be propitious to the essential superficiality of the greening green that does not seek the ultimate satisfaction in a coming to fruition. The hymns shed the informative (or, in technical terms, the constative) function of language in favor of singing the praises of Jesus and Mary, God the Father and the Holy Spirit, the saints and the church. Apparently ornamental, they let language flourish and blossom without forcing it to bear fruit.

Second, deeply engrained differences among plant parts, especially those relevant to the physical and metaphysical distinction between surface and depth, vanish as soon as one surveys them with the fresh gaze of *viriditas*. Regarded from the middle that is not swallowed up in the end, with the energy of greening greenness surging in the measure in which it is "realized," a fruit is as open as a leaf. The unbolting of the gates at the dawn of another day may be down to a perspectival switch from the fetish of a deep essence, withdrawn and enclosed in itself, to essence's gleaming on the surface of things, *à fleur de peau*.

How far are we from the verge? How close to it? Have we ever left it behind? Is it still ahead, an impending actuality? Do the signposts *ahead* and *behind* still make sense within the dynamics of verging?

Despite an encroaching geophysical and existential desert, *ariditas* is not yet victorious, and it doesn't have to be. While we are living (which means—beyond the biological, psychological, social, and spiritual processes connected to multiple registers of life—while we are repeatedly and often unawares touching and being touched on the verge of nonlife by a revitalizing freshness, which is not new but, precisely, the renewing and the renewed), there is still some *viriditas* in us. There is vegetality and divinity in us, the one passing into the other in all their sublimated, sublime, and ineluctably perverse guises. Life remains powerfully virginal and fragilely virile *on* the verge that is *in* us. But the flexibility of the virginal verge is not infinite: life's stunning capacity for self-reinvention may, more or less abruptly, come to a nonfruitful and nonflourishing end. The question for today—for *our* today, a verge very different from Hildegard's dawn—is how to hear the voice of freshness, with which ears to receive it, when desert aridity verges on a final triumph, when the flourishing verge is on the verge of extinction.

ANALOGIES

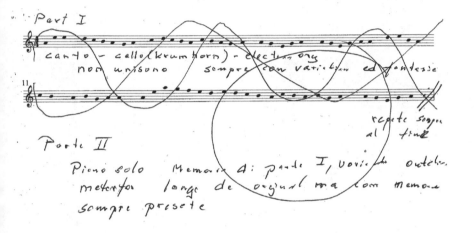

This movement, which comprises two parts, is an unstable
search. The first part circulates like a raga, where each voice tries
to find its own position in a common space. The second part,
which partially overlaps with the first, is more like an individual
rotation that seeks an eternity in its diminishing listening.

4 mins 56 secs

Analogies

Ancient thought abounded in analogies between seemingly disparate orders and kinds of existence. The microcosm and the macrocosm were seen as mirror images, reflecting the same underlying reality, contracted and amplified as the case might be. Perhaps the most influential of these accounts is the psycho-politics Plato sketches out in book 4 of his *Republic*. There, aspects of political organization tally with parts of the psyche: the appetites are the lot of the workers, *thumos* (usually rendered as "spiritedness") is a focal point of the warrior class (the guardians), and reason is the mark of philosopher-kings. The optimal state of the soul and of the polity is one where the three parts join forces and work in concert, in synergy or in alliance (*summachon* [440b]). For the alliance to be operative, spirit, represented in politics by the guardians, must take the side of reason, that is, of the rulers, repulsing the sway of the appetites and the masses but taking care not to alienate them. Should this delicate balancing act be successful, each sector of the psycho-political assemblage would perform its functions well, ensuring the maintenance of differences among parts for the good of each and of the whole.

At the physiological level, too, the microcosm and the macrocosm stood in a precise analogy to one another. In the bodies and senses of living beings (humans not excepted) ancient Greeks sighted the combinations and temporary delimitations of the immense elements that made up the outside world: fire, water, earth, and air. According to their line of argument, the sense of vision is possible by virtue of the eye housing a small portion of fiery brilliance, which, rushing to meet the fire that reigns in the world, is reunited with its native element. The health and constitution of the body are comprehensible through the humors and their balanced or unbalanced blending (*krâsis*). Empedocles was the first Greek thinker to identify the four elements, which he vegetalized, calling them "roots" (*rhizōmata*) (Simplicius, *Physics* 157–59). In the Hippocratic tradition, the work titled *On the Nature of Man* by Polybus details the four humors— phlegm, blood, yellow bile, and black bile—in parallel to the elements (V.1–4). Aristotle, in *On Generation and Corruption*, attributes to the elements physical characteristics—for example, fire is hot and dry, while earth is cold and dry (331a–b)—that could then be transposed onto the states of healthy and sick bodies.

Thermal psycho-physics is crucial to the theory of vegetal life that Hildegard delineates in her *Physica* and to its bearing on human corporeality. Throughout the treatise, she characterizes plants as either hot (*calida*) or cold (*frigida*), such that "the heat of the herbs signifies the spirit [*animam*], and the cold, the body [*corpus*]" (*Physica* Praef; *PL* 197:1127a). (One might say, with one eye to Aristotle and the other to Hildegard, that spirit is fiery and the body is earthy.) So, for instance, rye "is hot, but colder than wheat, and it has plenty of powers [*multas vires habet*]" (*Physica* I; *PL* 197:1130a). The medicinal and dietary properties of plants are indicative of how, starting from their own psycho-physiological makeup, they regulate the balance of heat and cold, of bodily and spiritual realities, in a human patient. In keeping with ancient thought, they fine-tune the humors and adjust our elemental composition, warding off its extravagances and immoderations, whether by putting an end to dangerous inflammations or by preventing the dissipation of spiritual heat in the coolness of the body.

But there is more to the curative qualities of vegetation in Hildegard's system than appears at first blush, and more, also, than is explicable through a simple carryover of ancient medical and physiological perspectives to medieval European worldviews. In particular, two idiosyncrasies of her approach stand out in an attentive observer's theoretical field of vision.

1. Hildegard is loath to exclude the plant kingdom from the spiritual sphere: physically expressed in heat, the powers (*vires*) of plants are the metaphysical reverberations of their *anima*—the animating principle, translatable as "soul" and, later on, "mind." Such powers belong under the heading of *viriditas*, of the "greening green," the self-refreshing capacity of finite existence, originally formulated with respect to vegetal life. Hildegard's plants are the vanguard of a convoluted, convulsed process, whereby physical qualities undergo spiritualization and spiritual realities are subject to physicalization. It is thanks to them that human "powers" are maintained and cherished at the cusp of medicine and theology.

2. The crafting of the first humans out of earth makes them plantlike, as the opening sentence in *Physica* states (*In creatione hominis de terra* . . .). It is from earth that humans and plants have imbibed their *viriditas*, each partaking of the universal capacity in a singular way: "And the earth gave its greening green [*et terra dabat viriditatem suam*] according to the kind, nature, customs, and all the specific circumstances of the humans" (*Physica* Pref; *PL* 197:1125a). Whereas, at its origins, humanity soaked *viriditas* up directly from the earth and on a par with the vegetation that sprouted from the terrestrial womb, the subsequent generations had to rely on the plants they consumed to keep receiving the gift of the greening green. The nourishing bodies of plants and the nutritive faculty of the vegetative soul became the bridges between "us" and the very thing (or nonthing) that keeps "us" alive. True to the offering of the earth, plants continued growing in a context-sensitive way, which apportioned to them the singular

universality of *viriditas*. In this, they embodied the activity of the Holy Spirit as the common "root . . . in every creature [*radix . . . in omni creatura*]" (*Symph.* 24.3).

The way Hildegard handles vegetal life is analogical and nonanalogical all at once. The provenance of humans and plants from earth (the Hebrew *adamah*), from which Adam even derives his name, as Hildegard herself notes, means that the likenesses between tree sap and blood, plant fibers and veins, the harmfulness of some herbs and diabolical types of behavior, and so forth hark back to a shared cause, at least when it comes to the formal and material types of causality in Aristotle. At this nonanalogical level, parts of different biological orders are expressions of the same underlying reality.

The physical aspects of life are signs for the corresponding regions of the spiritual world, since the soul "shows its powers according to the powers of the body [*secundum vires corporis vires suas ostendit*]" (*Scivias* I.4.17; CCCM 43, pp. 78–79). Along the same lines, the sun is a symbol for the Son of God, and the moon for the Church: *Sol autem significat Filium meum . . . Sed luna Ecclesiam . . . designat* (*Scivias* II.5; CCCM 43, p. 176). Although in corporeal existence heat stands for spirit and cold for the body, the distance between them dwindles once they are understood as physical qualities expressing metaphysical insights. They are the terms of comparison: cold is the privation of heat, just as bodily phenomena are deficient with respect to the powers of the soul they designate. Despite their frailty, however, the powers of the body are indispensable, because, without them, those of the soul would not have manifested themselves in the realm of appearance and, instead, would have stayed hidden like a potential plant concealed in a seed or in a dormant root. The bodily sign, the body *as* a sign, lends effectiveness to the nonbodily entity it signifies; the body is that according to which the soul shows (*ostendit*) itself and is discernible. This effectiveness is the power of power, the actuality that shepherds purely spiritual causes out of their isolation in the virtual sphere of essence.

In Hildegard's phenomenological psycho-physiology, the powers of the soul express themselves in the powers of the body indexed to that kind of soul. Thus, "in a person's infancy it [the soul—MM] produces simplicity, in youth—strength, and in adulthood, with all the person's veins full, it demonstrates its strongest powers in wisdom [*fortissimas vires suas in sapientia declarat*], as the tree in its first shoots is tender and then shows that it can bear fruit, and finally, in its full usefulness, bears it" (*Scivias* I.4.17; CCCM 43, p. 79). A demonstrative declaration of wisdom in a ripe fruit belongs together with the fleshy phenomenology of ostentation, "showing" the powers of the soul in the body. If there is an analogy here, it is not between plant and human souls or plant and human bodies, but between signs for the powers of the soul in the bodies of humans and plants.

At their peak (already anticipating a decline, to be sure), the workings of vitality in a human result in wisdom (*sapientia*), which, rather than the perfection of a disembodied mind, is the culmination of the physiological developmental arc extending from infant "simplicity" through adult physical strength to a true maturity. The same principle activated in a tree attains its maximum physical expression in a fruit that supersedes the simplicity of the seed and the ramified exuberance of vegetal growth. Viewed from the perspective of diverse existences, according to which the powers of this principle are uniquely calibrated, the analogy is between wisdom and fruit; considered from the vantage of *Scivias* and the revealed wisdom of the visions collected in it, the analogous elements are the orders of souls and bodies that are much more internally homogeneous than we tend to imagine.

Against the background of psycho-physical unity, it is hard to miss the Plotinian underpinnings of Hildegard's analogies (and nonanalogies). For Plotinus, the entire world, depicted as a gigantic tree, consisted in the ramifications of the One, thinking itself in the most varied shapes and processes into existence. When the One thought itself into being as growth in what Plotinus called *phutiké noesis,* the outcome was the kingdom of plants; sense-thought produced animals; and abstract thought was responsible for the human emanation of the One (*Enneads* II.8.8, 10–20). Possible parallels among modes of thinking and among their bodily expressions pointed back to a structured self-development of the One.

Nonetheless, between Plotinus and Hildegard, plants and humans switch places: for the Neoplatonist, the brightest thought is abstract cognition that grasps itself as thinking; for the Christian mystic, the greening green of *viriditas,* distributed into a whole range of powers, is apparent with the utmost vividness in plants. As Hildegard would elucidate them, the ramifications of the One are not yet wisdom, not yet maturity, but manifestations of the world's physical strength and ebullient proliferation. Plotinus must have had a premonition of theoretical trouble lurking in his attribution of the dimmest thinking to vegetal growth-thought, because, contemplating the One in his own manner (that is, exercising the capacity of abstract thought to think itself), he bestowed the shape of a tree onto the object of his contemplation. Giving voice to a similar intuition, Hildegard notes that "the soul's powers are like the form of a tree [*quasi arboris forma*]" (*Scivias* I.4.26; CCCM 43, p. 84).

❧

Besides a series of psycho-physiological correspondences, we find in Hildegard's corpus a hagiography and a theography mapped onto parts of plants in a kind of spiritual botany. The analogies mixed with the nonanalogical expressions of *viriditas* are complex, insofar as they involve various species of plants and plant organs, psychic faculties, and chief actors in Judeo-Christian theologies.

A salient example: while Hildegard correlates the Holy Spirit to a root shared by all creatures, she also contends that, as a rational animal, the human being "acts rationally, which is the first root fixed by the grace of God in every human [*rationabiliter operatur, quod est prima radix quam gratia Dei fixit in omnem hominem*]" (*Scivias* III.5.32; CCCM 43, p. 430). Like the Holy Spirit, rational action is a universal root, operative in all, even if the scope of its operations is limited to "all humans," while that of the Holy Spirit extends to the breath of life in "all creatures." The root is an anchor and a subterranean organ of nourishment for the entire plant. Deeper than and prior to the actual radicle, the Holy Spirit is the ontological fulcrum and source of sustenance for plants and other beings. It anchors beings in being, which in medieval thought is God. As for Hildegard's vision of human roots, it seems to replicate Plato's view in *Timaeus* that we are "heavenly plants," "for it is by suspending our head and root from that region whence the sustenance of our soul first came that the divine power keeps upright our whole body" (90a–b). Except that the rational root in Hildegard passes not only through the head but also through the hand, grounding humanity in doing, in the practical use of reason, to which "rational action" points, instead of tethering the human to the purely theoretical eidetic sphere.

We've had a glimpse of the Virgin Mary's vegetal figuration. She is a branch—"the greenest branch [*viridissima virga*]" (*Symph.* 19.1)—and the branch, in turn, evokes intellect in Hildegard's psychology: "the intellect in the soul is like the *viriditas* of branches and foliage on a tree" (*Scivias* I.4.26; CCCM 43, p. 84). A far cry from a prejudiced construction of fragile and unstable femininity, Mary is a firm aerial support for the leaves and flowers (above all, the Flower) she carries, and it is in a kindred sense that she is the figure of the intellect in Hildegard's tableau of a theologico-botanical psycho-physiology.

The intellect is the ability to discern differences, to distinguish among and select from a vast array of alternatives. Similar to rational conduct, it does not take effect in theoretical ideation; "the intellect in the soul" comes replete with concrete contents, among which one chooses, just as "the *viriditas* of branches" (and, especially, "the greenest branch") appears before the senses not in the wintry bareness of abstraction but covered with leaves. Exactly how intellect is a facet of the soul most appropriate to the Virgin becomes clear once we give prominence to the notion that virginity for the sake of total devotion to God is, in the eyes of Hildegard, a spiritual *choice*, the highest discernment, requiring tremendous fortitude if it is to be made repeatedly, reaffirmed in the face of temptation. The power of the intellect is a link in the semantic and conceptual chain, where *viriditas* is intercalated with virginity, vigor, and virility.

Further surprising and upending our gender stereotypes, Hildegard correlates Christ to a flower, which "arose in an unplowed field, a flower [*flos*] so excellent that it will never wither from any accident of mortality, but in full *viriditas* will last forever" (*Scivias* II.6.26; CCCM 43, p. 253). The flower is analogous to the will—"the will like its [the tree's] flowers [*voluntas autem quasi flores in ea*]" (*Scivias* I.4.26; CCCM 43, p. 84)—which molds the power to act, determining it one way or another, and is also molded by these very determinations. A reasonable will relies on the discernments provided by the intellect for its resolution and self-determination. But the support it receives from these discernments cannot be compared to standing on a flat rock, extraneous to whomever or whatever it provides with a hard mineral foundation.

The will grows out of the intellect, which nourishes and supports it. The intellect carries the will as a branch carries its flower or as Mary carries her Son. There is undeniable continuity between the carrying and the carried, to the point where the one passes into and for the other, the intellect blossoming into the will, the branch bursting in flowers, Mary's virginity issuing forth in the Child outside the confines of productive (or reproductive) sexuality. Ideally, this multifaceted continuity is protected from disruptions signaled by the eventual fall of the flower or of the fruit it may metamorphose into in the botanical domain. In actuality, though, ruptures, disconnections, distractions, and other interferences are rife. Rather than a static, eternal, incorruptible will, the excellence of Christ the Flower's unperturbed *viriditas* implies the will's fresh commitment—self-refreshing across all the discontinuities, doubts, and crises—to redeem creation, to reinvigorate the quasi-divine capacity of creation to renew itself.

❧

I pause my fledgling exposition of vegetal psycho-physio-theology here, so as to take up two climacteric objections. Whoever would voice the first of these would rightly note that Hildegard's tripartite analogies are volatile, their elements changeable from one work to the next and, at times, within the same manuscript. For instance, a theological equivalent of roots shifts from the Holy Spirit in *Scivias* to the patriarchs and the prophets, whom Hildegard hails as "the happy roots [*felices radices*]" in *Symphonia* (32.1). The Virgin, who in these works has appeared as a green branch, is analogized, in *Scivias* as well, to grass: "My Son was born of the incorrupt virgin, who knew nothing of any pain, but remained in the fresh purity of her integrity, like grass that flourishes in verdant glory [*in gloria viriditatis*] when the dew falls on it from Heaven" (*Scivias* II.6.25; CCCM 43, p. 255). This vegetal personification, reminiscent of Tertullian and Irenaeus, accords with the view of Christ's birth as a flower that cropped up in an unplowed field, not with one that blossomed on the greenest branch. Then, on another occasion, the relation between the Mother and the Child is imagined "as balsam [that] oozes from a tree [*ut balsamum ex arbore sudat*]" (*Scivias* II.3.13; CCCM 43, p. 142). What is going on here?

One can plausibly explain each modification by exercising strict exegetical discipline and hermeneutical vigilance in the context of the passages where it arises. The case of roots is remarkably instructive in this regard. If the root ultimately grows at the nexus of universality and singularity, of the Holy Spirit (or rational action) and all creatures (or all humans), then it is not a matter of indifference whether analysis begins at the universal or the singular end of the relation. An analogue of the root, the Holy Spirit is the universal breath of life, received in a singular fashion by each creature. The patriarchs and the prophets are, conversely, singular individuals, the more or less accidental genealogical and theological-political roots that are universalized by virtue of their faith, visionary messages, or foundational acts.

Divergences between the singular and the universal points of departure apply, likewise, to rational deeds that represent, in Hildegard's montage of mental faculties and behaviors, the psychic roots of humanity. Consistent with the primacy of the Holy Spirit, abstract rationality may impel a deed, assisting in its development from the embryonic stage (the initial resolve of the will) onward. At the other end of the spectrum, commencing from a singularity set on the path to universality, a deed may aspire to rationality as its end. The beginning is complicated also for the very simple reason that a journey may get under way from more than one threshold or verge. After all, the *arkhé* of the patriarchs is also the *first* root.

Such exegetical overtures are bound to run into formal and material limits. The Virgin Mary's transformation from a green branch into verdant grass still makes sense when grafted onto an inner change in the spiritual geometry of Hildegard's text: superseding the verticality of the tree, on which the branch grows (the genealogical Tree of Jesse, on the one hand, and the Tree of Redemption that inverts the fructiferous variety, which instigated the Fall, on the other), is the immense divide between the grass stretching out below and the heavenly expanse above. There is a subtle move from immanence to transcendence in this transformation, from the uninterrupted course of ramified vertical and horizontal lines to the gap between what is above and what is below, traversed only by the dew that precipitates the immaculate conception and that, in the Judeo-Christian tradition, signals the resurrection of the dead. But set the other vegetal transcriptions of Mary and Jesus—say, into a tree and its sap—side by side with the relevant psychic analogy, and the already overstretched exegetical imagination will tear! In keeping with a reading procedure guided by the ideal of consistency, the statement, "The soul in the body is like sap in a tree [*anima in corpore est velut sucus in arbore*]" (*Scivias* I.4.26; CCCM 43, p. 84), would turn Jesus into the soul, Mary into the body, her virginal conception into an event of her "ensoulment," and Christ's birth into death, the soul leaving the body. That is one of many *material* limits to understanding and interpretation as far as the workings of Hildegard's analogical apparatus are concerned.

A *formal* limit to the search for constancy and consistency among the analogies is drawn by the method readers follow and, consciously or unconsciously, ascribe to Hildegard herself. In the midst of their own projections, they (we) forget that her thought is not set in stone. It is futile to look up to it for solid connections and immutable shapes, akin to those making up Kant's table of judgments, the categories, or schemata. Rather than a defect, the fluidity of her psycho-physio-theology befits a methodology in tune more with vegetal processes than with the mineral world, itself subject to erosion, sedimentation, and diagenesis. Rather than a neat grid of inorganic parallels, analogies and nonanalogies are a tangle, reminiscent of a rhizome. The elasticity and, indeed, the plasticity of Hildegard's visions is the elasticity and plasticity of plant ontology.

Parts of plants rarely remain the same as they grow, metamorphose, or simply fall off from their living host. The psychic, physical, and theological sections of Hildegard's "taxonomy," too, grow into and out of one another, interchangeable in their uniqueness. The rapid multiplication of analogies (and nonanalogies), with religious figures or plant parts reiterated in a large array of combinations, conforms to modular growth that proceeds by repetition and is redolent, at the same time, of a mindboggling diversity of vegetal shapes, colors, and sizes. (It bears noting that Hildegard associates these "sense data," pertaining to the tree of the soul, with the human senses. The association does not just articulate the objective and the subjective dimensions of the senses; it goes a step further and expresses the human subject through the empirical variations of its vegetal object.) Hence, the formal limit to system-building on the basis of Hildegard's writings is an enabling one: as soon as one engages with her work, one quickly intuits that the outlines of her method are as vegetal (mutable, metamorphosing, growing, decaying . . .) as the message it conveys.

The second objection has to do with the role of fruits, including fruit-bearing capacities, in the analogies. I have touched upon this issue in the previous chapter; in the present one, it flares up with new urgency. Given that neither Mary nor Jesus is compared to a fruit—the one is akin to a branch, the other to a flower—they are debarred from wisdom, to which this plant organ alludes. A fruit is the mature expression of planthood, coming on the heels of buds and flowers, while wisdom is the mature expression of humanity. Thus, Mary and Jesus, and, with them, the very kernel of Christianity, are cardinally immature.

You may consequently wonder: is maturity such a desirable thing? The fruit is where plant being is at its crest, the ascending curve all but finished and the phase of its decline and decay about to set in. In human old age, as Hildegard relates right after the fruit analogy, "the soul's powers are gentler, as if from a weariness at human knowledge [*velut in taedio scientiae hominis ostendit*]; as when winter approaches the sap of the tree diminishes in the branches and the leaves" (*Scivias* I.4.17; CCCM 43, p. 79). Maturity is a precursor of rotting away. Mary and Jesus rebel against its inexorability as they welcome *viriditas* and shun the fully grown, ripe old age of the fallen world. An intellect and a will more astute than conventional wisdom, they extend themselves, open up to exteriority as a leafy branch and a flower, basking in the promise of life and spring. Anachronistically examined through this lens, Protestantism at *its* roots revived the inaugural immaturity of Christianity after its institutional fruit had grown overripe.

Jesus's vegetal analogues in Hildegard's oeuvre bypass the fruit, preceding it in the form of the grapevine flower and succeeding it in the shape of the grape's fermentation in wine. Bread is the afterlife of wheat, wine is the afterlife of grapes, the eucharistic body and blood having left the state and the stage of decay behind. In a double viticultural analogy evincing the modular growth of Hildegard's text, God the Father is the vine out of which the wine that is his Son flows (*ut vinum de vite sudat, ita et Filius meus de corde meo exivit*), and the Son himself is "liquor from the sweetest and strongest fruit [*sucus de dulcissimo ac fortissimo fructu vitis*]" of "all merciful and true justice" (*Scivias* II.6.28; CCCM 43, p. 257). Having overcome death, the fermented products of vegetal afterlife, including alcoholic spirits, border on spirit. In *Physica*, grapevine (*vitis*) anticipates the spiritualization of the body suffused with the heat of spirit. It is said to have "fiery heat and moisture in it. The fire is so strong as to change its sap into a flavor that other trees and herbs do not have" (*Physica* I, liv; *PL* 197:1244b). The medicinal properties of the plant are also conducive to the reversal of decay: the warm ashes of grapevine submerged in wine are supposed to help cure "flesh rotting around one's teeth" (*Physica* I, liv; *PL* 197:1244c).

Occasionally, vegetal metamorphoses in Hildegard's analogies correlate Jesus to fruit, notably "the strongest fruit [*fortissimus fructus*] that shall never fail" (*Scivias* II.6.32; CCCM 43, p. 261). Does this mean that the rebellion of Christianity against mature wisdom ends in defeat? Not quite. Mutation into any plant part, including the fruit, is the inalienable possibility of Hildegard's living thought, so long as its mutability is not absorbed into an ideally immutable end, to which the teleological whole would be oriented as one. Becoming-fruit is not a coveted goal but yet another point of transition when overviewed from the perspective of *viriditas* with its open-endedness and potentialities for self-renewal reversing the movement of ripening and decay, particularly by moving through decay to life itself. In addition, Jesus's identification with fruit is highly qualified in the passage in question. The full sentence from *Scivias* reads: "And as bread [*panis*] nourishes people, the Son of God nourishes believers in faith, for He is the strongest fruit that shall never fail." As bread, his eucharistic body is the fermented "fruit" of wheat, in which decay has been overcome along with the tedium of human knowledge past its prime. A leap from flower freshness to a vegetal afterlife imbued with spirit happens imperceptibly, the fruit dissolving in the flexible power of *viriditas*.

Whereas the overall psychic corollary to a fruit is wisdom, Hildegard is careful to separate the early from the late varieties and to assign appropriate human manifestations to each. The mind, she insists, "is truly like the first bursting out of fruit [*animus vero velut primus erumpens fructus*]," and reason "is like a perfectly mature fruit [*ratio autem quasi fructus eius in maturitate perfectus*]" (*Scivias* I.4.26; CCCM 43, p. 84). What explains this hairsplitting differentiation?

The mind (*animus*) is the yet undetermined, or underdetermined, conjunction of faculties and capacities to cognize the world. It is best understood as the principle of a uniquely human life, nearly identical to the human soul (*anima*). Even young children have a mind, which some in the early modernity have read as a blank slate, a *tabula rasa*. By contrast, reason takes time to develop, to be honed in a habitual practice of reasonable conduct, to slowly garner its juices from the accumulation of life experiences. With reason, the mind receives the richness of its determinations, swapping the state of mere potentiality for actuality, just as a fruit gradually gains its recognizable shapes and colors in ripeness. Wisdom is the culmination of this process, the fruit of fruit as it were, the yield of a mind that learns to reason and grows to be reasonable.

Human roots and fruits end up being caught in a virtuous circle, reason obtaining nourishment from rational action, which activates in practice the mere principle of rationality.

The next question is who the theological analogue of the fruit is. Hildegard's shocking answer: the devil. "Diabolic persuasion," *diabolica persuasio*, inclines Adam to taste the forbidden fruit and be poisoned by its sweetness: "For in the taste of the fruit he knew by disobedience, a harmful sweetness [*nociva dulcedo*] poured itself into his blood and flesh, producing the corruption of vice. And, therefore, I feel the sin of the flesh [*peccatum carnis*] in me, but intoxicated by wrongdoing [*per culpam inebriata sum*], I neglect the purest God" (*Scivias* I.4.5; CCCM 43, p. 68).

A fruit is fleshy and sweet in the state of ripeness, when it is apt for digestion and for dispensing its wisdom. Thereafter, it lapses into overripeness, the harbinger of decrepitude and decay, replicated in the weariness and tedium of the wise. The marks that decay mercilessly leaves on human and vegetal flesh are the signs of an imminent end, of irreversible finality even, in the eyes of nonbelievers and sinners, who, as Hildegard has it, "neglect the purest God," because they are committed to the flesh as the be-all and end-all of existence, cut off from the spirit that animates it. A decaying fruit is, for its part, still bristling with *viriditas* in anticipation of another beginning as it nourishes the seed, now primed for germination. The issue, therefore, is not decay *per se* but its unhitching from growth and association with the end. An alternative vision is required to register the positivity of decay, the vision that, not totally mired in the flesh and its sin, takes a second, panoramic look at the larger vegetal process and at the analogous spiritual course, without missing the floral preexistence and the fermenting afterlife of fruits. "Diabolic persuasion" puts the fruit's *before* and *after* (the moments Hildegard privileges in her analogy to Jesus) out of sight. The "corruption of vice" displaces and eternalizes the temporal corruption of the flesh, which, on its neglected upside, concocts fertile grounds for future growth—biological and spiritual.

As far as the translation of the fruit into psychic processes is concerned, Adam and Eve are guilty of impetuousness. By eating from the Tree of Knowledge of Good and Evil, they desire to gain direct access to a wisdom not rooted in rational action and detached from the cumulative growth that experiential maturation affords. The fruit they grasp following an apparent shortcut is simultaneously unripe and overripe, unsustainable for the branch/intellect saddled with the green issue of an underdetermined mind. Hildegard goes as far as to suggest that, in their haste, the first humans did not even properly taste the forbidden fruit and certainly did not digest it: "for they tried to know the wisdom of the law with their intelligence, as if with the nose, but did not perfectly digest it by putting it in their mouths, or fulfil it in full blessedness by the work of their hands . . . For, by the Devil's counsel [*consiliante diabolo*], they turned their back on divine command and sank into the gaping mouth of death [*in maximus rictus mortis*]" (*Scivias* II.1.8; CCCM 43, p. 117).

The aesthetic superficiality of smelling and tasting without digesting the fruit/wisdom when time itself is not yet ripe spells out not only impetuousness but also, in terms of its consequences, an upheaval and reversal in the relation between the digesting and the digested. Adam and Eve are swallowed up by that which they intend to swallow, dragged down into the abyss of death, yawning in the dark pit of an enormous impersonal mouth—unless they are immediately incorporated into the cavernous space of death's hungry belly. That an abyss opens up on the surface of the taste buds (elsewhere in *Scivias* Hildegard calls upon readers to conquer in themselves "what was sown in the lust of sin by the taste of the fruit [*ex gustu pomi*]" [*Scivias* I.2.24; CCCM 43, p. 30]) is another piece of corroborating evidence for the vegetality of sin and redemption. What is vitally important to plants resides on their ontic and ontological surfaces, on the unfurled leaf, a blossoming flower, or a sensitive root tip, through which the entire vegetal being extends toward its other (light, the elements, insects, and so forth). Vitality is, as Hildegard has disclosed, concentrated in the color green, abounding with life itself. The superficiality of taste, contrasted to the depth of digestion, is homologous to the primacy of appearance over a hidden essence in vegetality. Not to be dismissed as ornamental additions to a rational being that is the human, the senses—including the gustatory—are the surfaces that make us who we are. So, the tasting of fruity sweetness has a bearing on the Fall.

There is a memorable theological precedent to the about-face of digestion in the Christian tradition, albeit in a diametrically opposed context. I am referring to Augustine's take on communion. Ventriloquizing Jesus, he proclaims in his *Confessions*: "I am the food of the fully grown; grow and you will feed on me. And you will not change me into you, like the food your flesh eats, but you will be changed into me" (VII.x.16). To consume the body of Christ is to be metabolized and incorporated into divine existence; to eat of the forbidden fruit is to be absorbed into death and inexistence. Whatever the extent of its sublimation, spiritualization, and divinization, digestion is a feature of the Aristotelian *to threptikon*, the vegetal vital principle that conjoins the capacities for nourishment and reproduction. Regardless of a reversal in the roles played by the eater and the eaten, their relation is assimilated to vegetal dynamics and mechanisms. To speak of digestion theologically is to digest virtue and sin, God and the devil, into plant being.

Skipping back from the fruit to the flower, we may recall that Jesus blossomed either on the greenest branch or in an unplowed green field that was Mary. In the latter scenario, he was "a flower born in a field though its seed was never sown there [*flos nascitur in agro non seminatus semine*]" (*Scivias* III.8.15; CCCM 43, p. 497). A wildflower, then. There is no labor involved in his conception or birth, neither the labor that signifies work nor the labor that refers to parturition, a double absence coded as good.

How to square this image with Hildegard's critique of those "fruitless plants that spring up easily [*facile nascuntur*] by themselves from the ground," seeing that "the fruit-bearing varieties must be sown and planted with great labor [*magno labore*]" (*Scivias* III.9.20; CCCM 43, p. 532)? Such plants are weeds (*inutilis herba*) in her psycho-physio-theological taxonomy, the vile members of a community who outnumber the virtuous and "surpass them in power." Rooted in themselves alone, in their own capricious will and indeterminate desire, they are uprooted not only from God ("not rooted in my planting or by the touch of knowledge of my gift and my decree [*Non mea plantatione aut tactu cognitionis doni mei aut ordinationis meae radicati*]" [*Scivias* III.9.20; CCCM 43, p. 533]) but also from the rational practice that anchors the human. The highest and the lowest, the Flower of redemption and weeds, converge on untilled grounds, in their exemption from work.

In biblical text, labor is one of the punishments God meted out to Adam for the original sin. Agricultural work offers solutions to life's problems that pose problems of their own. It transposes life's precariousness onto its interaction with the environment, forces human beings to keep close to the soil, which frequently will not respond to their exertions, until the final moment when they return to the earth as corpses (Gen. 3:19). The burden is the one Jesus eases, redeeming sinful humanity by breaking "the tree of Adam's death and perdition [*arborem mortis et perditionis Adae*]" (*Scivias* III.6.35; CCCM 43, p. 461). (Following another, equally vegetal, rendition of the event, Jesus does not break the tree that sparked off the original sin but substitutes for it the tree of the cross.) In other words, Jesus obviates work; his birth, life, and even death are the supreme play—free of labor, yet absolutely serious and passionate, solemn in their heralding of sabbatical existence. Those who refuse hard work out of the sheer stubbornness of their fickle wills also engage in play in violation of God's punishing command and without the burden having been lifted by redemptive self-sacrifice.

Labor is bookended, therefore, on the one side by the paradisiac leisure Christianity seeks to recover and on the other by the laziness of the apostate, uprooted from divine and human grounds for sustainable growth.

Physica interprets agricultural labor in light of the contribution such work makes to vegetal "goodness" and utility. "Plants which are sown by human labor [*per laborem hominis seminantur*]," Hildegard writes in that manual, "and spring up and grow gradually, are like domestic animals which are nourished with care in the home. By the labor with which they are planted and cultivated, they throw off the acidity and bitterness of their moisture" (*Physica* I, Praef.; *PL* 197:1126b). Within Hildegard's theologically inflected natural history, the interval between the Fall and salvation requires the ongoing work of restoring the earth's *viriditas*, of purifying the earth's emissions, transforming them from the terrestrial "sweat" (*sudor*) that irrigates harmful plants to "moisture" and "juice," *humor* and *sucus*, that bring forth beneficial plants and fruit-bearing trees (*Physica* I, Praef.; *PL* 197:1126b). The earth is purified by tending to what grows upon it, provided that it is cultivated "with care" (*cum sollicitudine*), allotting enough time for plants to attain *their* good, which is also that of the earth that bears them.

In anticipation of Jesus's own blossoming, agricultural work is the scaled-down, labor-intensive, unremitting, caring redemption of the earth, its sweat mirroring the sweat of Adam's brow, with which he and his descendants gain their daily bread. Lest we push the comparison too far, our sweat is not merely analogous to that of the earth, transmuted into moisture and juice thanks to the expenditure of human efforts. Once redeemed in the Sabbath of existence, the divine curse lifted, the earth and the human will stop sweating. Freedom hinges on redemption *through* work and on the redemption *of* work, with plants and the earth for our partners in the emancipatory venture.

Hildegard reads the human as a small facsimile of the world. She notes: "the human contains in itself the likeness of heaven and earth [*homo similitudinem caeli et terrae continet in se*]" (*Scivias* II.1.2; CCCM 43, p. 113). This likeness—or these likenesses: two in one and one in two—are the soul and the body, the "circle, which contains clarity, breath and rationality as the sky has its lights, air and winged creatures [*volatilia*]" and "the receptacle containing humidity, germination, and birth, as the earth has its fertility, fruition, and animals" (*Scivias* II.1.2; CCCM 43, p. 113). Plants and animals, with the exception of birds and perhaps winged insects, are relegated to the earthly domain, placed outside the bright and airy expanses of the soul. But the human does not hover above the terrestrial fold, either. Our position is more ambivalent, since we contain both the likeness of heaven and that of the earth, shared with other forms of life. Our psychophysicality is such that our bodies and souls capture what is above and what is below: each of us stands at the intersection of darkness and light, a humid receptacle touching and being touched by the circle of airy lucidity.

As Hildegard will realize while elaborating her vegetal analogies, plants are no worse than humans in spanning the heavenly and the earthly realms, inasmuch as they strive to the clarity of light above and to the humidity and the cradle of germination below. Rather than banish plants from the circle of ensouled beings, Hildegard will acknowledge that they are at the core of the human soul, exclaiming: "Understand, O human, what you are in your soul [*Unde, o homo, intellege quid in anima tua sis*]!" at the conclusion of her intricate soul–tree analogy (*Scivias* I.4.26; CCCM 43, p. 84). She will give the Socratic injunction, *Know thyself!* received from the oracle at Delphi, a peculiar twist: *Know that you are a plant and know, furthermore, that your knowledge, hued with a fading green, is the afterglow of vegetal growth.*

RESONANCES

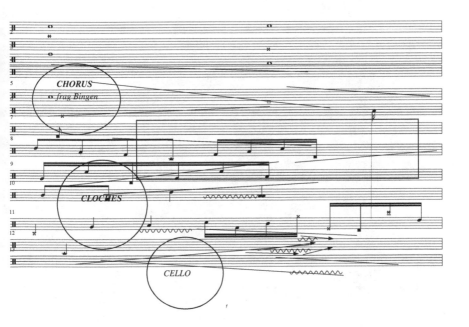

An attempt at approaching Hildegard's view of composition.
You can call it "symphony," as far as the shape and not just
the sound is concerned. There are echoes of times in different
spaces. The future will be the present and the present becomes
the future. Voices meet both the bells of time and the singing
of loneliness in separated tones from another space. Together,
these elements form a dreamlike state of uncertainty.

7 mins 08 secs

Resonances

Few people had a clearer sense of the vibrancy of being than Hildegard did. Or, more precisely, clearer senses. To recap: her notion of *viriditas*, the self-refreshing power of creation made visible in vegetation, is the greening green, vibrant and vibrating. In it, greenness is in equal measure metaphysical and physical, a possibility and an actuality, hidden and revealed, irradiating and absorbing intense light and sound waves, open not just to seeing and hearing but also to touching, smelling, tasting, to say nothing of the activity of greening that sees us, hears us, smells, tastes, and touches *us*. Experientially, it is a total synesthesia, the fusion of all the senses, metonymically consigned to vision, which is further represented by a unique section from the middle of the humanly visible spectrum: the color green. Ontologically, it encompasses what is given to the senses and the givenness of the senses themselves, along with the rest of the body–mind assemblage inspired and animated by *viriditas*. Human or not, life is a green mass, and that which enlivens it is a symphony in green.

In her famous letter to the prelates at Mainz, dating from 1178–79 and protesting the prohibition of musical liturgy in retribution for the burial of a heretic on monastery grounds, Hildegard advances her cosmological and theological theory of music. Pithily, she remarks: "the soul is symphonic [*symphonialis est anima*]" (*Epist*. XXIII, 141; CCCM 91, p. 65). The silencing of music is a brazen attack on the soul, which is thereby deprived of a chance to come to terms with its own structure in the acoustics of sounding-with. But this is not all. Because Hildegard's favorite analogy for the soul is a tree, we might say that the symphony is intravegetal in virtue of combining the vibrations of different, semi-autonomous organs of plants (branches, roots, trunks, leaves, flowers . . .) and their corresponding "mental faculties" (intelligence, wisdom, sensoriality . . .). An interdiction placed on musical liturgy disrupts the concerted growth, metamorphosis, decay, and regeneration of plant parts, reflected in the collaborative existence—the coexistence—of parts of the soul.

What to make of the soul's symphonicity? The Aristotelian insight that the human psyche is the interlacing of vegetal, animal, and "properly" human types of vitality implies, in keeping with Hildegard's intervention, that their joint operations produce the equivalent of musical harmony. Each organ, each instrument of the originally cleaved soul retains its singular voice and pitch, sounding at different frequencies and having distinct timbres. An extravegetal symphony, in which these instruments participate, does not annul the sonic differences among them; on the contrary, it builds on their heterogeneity so as to create a more intricate and robust, multilayered musical-existential composition. Nor is the *aggregate* of parts redundant. The being of the soul is symphonic: insofar as it is, the soul is a symphony; otherwise, it is nothing at all.

The symphony that is the soul orchestrates the relation of the soul and what is not a soul, the body. In an implicit meditation on the Greek *logos*, which may be translated, among many other possibilities, as "voice" and "reason," Hildegard writes in another letter: "The voice is body; rationality is the soul [*Vox est corpus, rationalitas anima*]" (*Epist*. XXXIr, 145; CCCM 91, p. 87). If "the voice is body," then the opposite is also true: every body is a voice, a voicing of existence in the creatures' acts of self-showing, self-signifying, giving signs of their being. The symphony is made of bodies/voices; yet, it is the soul that is symphonic, which means that the soul is an ensemble of voices, an articulation of bodies, the grammar of their jointure. That is where rationality (*rationalitas*) fits it. The word, as Hildegard hears it, is devoid of the arrogant overtones of an exclusively human quality taking over the entire domain of the soul. Instead, it denotes the *sym-* of *symphonia*, the connective "with," which strings bodies together, gathers the voices that they are into a chorus, and marks the passages from one sound to another. Rationality is relationality and, above all, the relation of bodies to themselves and to others. The rational soul is never in itself; it stretches between bodies—between human and human, human and vegetal, vegetal and animal, human and divine, vegetal and vegetal, vegetal and divine . . . This soul, then, is ecological.

The hypothesis concerning a symphonic connection between the body and the soul receives additional support from Hildegard's assertion: "The body is truly the garment of the soul, which has a living voice [*corpus vero indumentum est anime, que vivam vocem habet*], and so it is proper for the body, in harmony with the soul, to use its voice to sing praises to God" (*Epist.* XXIII, 129–31; CCCM 91, p. 64). Apparently superfluous, the worn more than the wearing, ready to be taken off as an unnecessary piece of clothing, the body joins the soul anyway, in a common song of praises to God. A garment outlines as much as it hides the shape of the one wearing it; the body hides and outlines the shape and the sound of the soul. Whereas the body is voice, the soul "has a living voice": the soul appropriates the voice that is the body and breathes life into it, renders the voice a living one. The soul *sounds the body*, as one would play a flute by blowing across the embouchure while opening and closing holes in the tube with one's fingers, and it *sounds with the body* in a symphonic arrangement. There is, moreover, no reason to believe that songs of praise to the creator are exclusively human. Other bodies and souls (not least, those of plants) participate in the symphony after their own manner, with living voices that might be foreign to the human template of vitality.

Liturgical music, or Boethius's *musica instrumentalis*, is on this view a replacement, poor though unassailably important, for the prelapsarian harmonies of existence (Boethius's *musica mundana*). After the Fall, Adam was deprived of "that angelic voice [*vocis angelice*] which he had in paradise" (*Epist.* XXIII, 71–72; CCCM 91, p. 63), making the subsequent recovery of music and song a nostalgic reminder of what had been irretrievably lost. *Musica instrumentalis* has a voice that is simultaneously living and not living, that substitutes for the unsubstitutable, that reminisces about life from and beyond the verge of death. Such a music is spectral.

Provided that the first humans had angelic voices, they also had angelic bodies (which they similarly lost), since the two—body and voice—are identical in the eyes of Hildegard. This inference is a long way from arguing that human corporeality was ethereal and altogether immaterial prior to the Fall. One should be mindful of the Greek etymology of *ángelos*, which refers to a messenger, a mediator, an intermediary in the act of sending, moving between the sending and the receiving. Angels are spiritual beings not because they are unencumbered by matter, but because spirit is the conductor of materiality, or, better, the intermateriality of ligaments, connective tissues, bonds, ties, relations putting matter in touch with itself. An angelic voice is the voice that carries the word of the other—or that falls silent so that the other's word would be able to resound. But, while the messenger of creation is human, its message is vegetal, that is, *viriditas*, the self-refreshing power of the greening green, turning generation and decay into regeneration, another germination and growth.

An echo of Boethius's *musica mundana* or *musica universalis*, more commonly known as the "music of the spheres," is perceptible in Hildegard's approach to "elemental harmony" (*harmonia el-ementorum*). In effect, what we are hearing is an echo in an echo, the one at the level of a formal resemblance between the two thinkers, the other at the level of content, where the microcosm reverberates with the macrocosm. The "symphonic voice of human spirit [*simphonialis vox spiritus hominis*]" is a resonance chamber for "the delightful and glorious sounds of the elements [*sonus elementorum iocundus et gloriosus*], emanating from the moving torrents of the superior ether, through which the firmament un-folds" (*TOQ* XXVII, *solutio*; CCCM 226A, p. 124). The audible is a vehicle for the inaudible—because situated either above or below the thresholds of our perception—vibrations of the universe.

Symphonic human spirit is a complex singularity: its constitu-tive connections (the *sym-*, or "with," of *symphonia*) forge links among human beings, phenomena, realities, on the one hand, and between these and an actuality beyond the human, on the other. So much so that the hard and fast partitions between these "between" and "among" collapse. The combined voices culled from a corner of the world sing the entire world. Human being-with borders on withness as such, not as a surreptitious means of imperialistically invading, processing, and appropriating that which is "not us," but as a way of welcoming incomparably larger domains, including the elements and divinity. Partaking in sono-rous spirit, which is often unfortunately muzzled, humans are probably more capacious still for the world than the world is for humans. Whatever remains of human spirit after the Fall remains angelic. Ecology is a symphony.

Hildegard closes *Scivias* with the quintessentially synesthetic "vision" of a symphony. There, she specifies that symphony is spirit: *symphonia autem spiritum* (III.13.12; CCCM 43, p. 614). The inheritor of Adam's lost angelic voice and the musical notion of the soul, symphonic spirit is nowhere near a purely ideal entity. It is the being-with of all the relations that bind bodies to souls, souls to souls, bodies to bodies, and, ultimately, the entire lot to the divine ground whence it arose. That "the voice of the multitude [*vox multitudinis*]" sounds "in a symphonizing harmony [*in harmonia symphonizans*]" (III.13; CCCM 43, p. 615) is a sign that the bodies/voices of a throng of creatures have forged a transspecies alliance stitched together with the connective threads of spirit. What follows this observation is the future core of Hildegard's *Symphonia*: fourteen songs glorifying the Virgin Mary, the saints, and other religious figures. Tellingly, the hymn *O tu suavissima virga frondens de stirpe Jesse* ("O, you, sweetest branch flourishing from the rootstock of Jesse") is called in the preamble to this auditory vision "the symphony of holy Mary [*symphonia de sancta Maria*]," which features a distinctly vegetal message. Symphonizing is not only humanizing but also vegetalizing, occasioning the concert of spirit under the auspices of *viriditas*.

In the register of *musica instrumentalis*, the praise due to God rolls off the strings of a harp, to the beats of timbrels and cymbals. But another mode of hearing is necessary to appreciate the symphony of existence, the hearing practiced by those who have "sharp ears [*acutas aures*]" capable of "inner discernments [*interioris intellectus*]" (III.1.18; CCCM 43, p. 347). That is the hearing attuned to *musica mundana*, the vibrations of the world too fine for a "normal" human ear. The hearing, or, rather, the listening, Hildegard advocates at the close of *Scivias* is not superhuman; it is not divine either, but vegetal, an acoustic tuning into the world with one's whole bodily extension, with the voice (which the body is) quieted down, stilled so as to hear everything and everyone else. Of all the creatures, in fact, plants have the sharpest ears, listening to vibrations above and below ground, even if their auditory organs are hardly recognizable as such by human standards. So, a book of mystical knowledge ends with an appeal to honing the powers of mystical hearing, themselves inherited from the plant kingdom.

❧

The opposite of merely decorative, Hildegard's musical order conveys "the justice of God [*iustitie Dei*]" (*Epist.* XXIII, 121; CCCM 91, p. 64). The ancient concept of justice as adjustment, being in tune, harmonization, the fittingness together of things is alive and well in her thought. Covibrations, resonances, symphonic sonorities are the phenomenal marks of this attuning and attuned fit. The basis of justice is the body vibrating with its soul and the soul with the body, the one suiting the other as a glove, or, precisely, as a suit, a piece of clothing (*indumentum*), in Hildegard's own words. Also just is the articulation of bodies, each with itself and with the others, that resonate on a consistent plane, adjusted to emitting and receiving multiple waves and frequencies across the relational gap. Finally (or initially—depending on how one sees it), "it is just that God is praised in all [*iustum est ut in omnibus laudetur Deus*]" (*Epist.* XXIII, 137; CCCM 91, p. 65).

The being of all creatures is their incomparable praise of God, the praise adjusted to their particular modes of being. Plants flourish and blossom; humans sing, their bodies/voices handed over to breath—the very "breath that God sent into a human body [*spiraculo quod Deus misit in corpus hominis*]" (*Epist.* XXIII, 136; CCCM 91, p. 65)—and distilled into sopranos and baritones, basses and contraltos. Plant flourishing is their song of praise; human song is our flourishing. Vegetal adjustment to the environment, which plants mold in a low key by creating microclimates around their ecosystems, is divine musical justice, the embodied expression of a fit (better: fittingness) that never stays the same, but, with each element running away from the other and catching up only for the other to escape, evolves almost like a fugue.

Besides instrumental music, acts of charity and good works praise God in a uniquely human fashion. These acts are in line with the mutual adjustment of plants and their worlds, as well as with musical harmonies that, with respect to the sonorous whole, string disparate sounds together. The coordination of good works aims at coordination as such, at the repair and adjustment of the world, or, in the Hebraic tradition, *tikkun olam*. More than healing, it sings the world and lets the world grow, binding its sundered parts together without hiding the sutures.

When Hildegard invokes in the same breath "the nature of spirit [*spiritus naturam*] as considered by the prophets" and "the nature of celestial harmony [*naturam celestis harmonie*] (*Epist.* XXIII, 139; CCCM 91, p. 65), she is hinting at the fittingness behind every actual fit, the justice of what is "just right" in its relation to the other. This fittingness, this justice, is spirit. Its activity and outcome are tantamount to a harmonious arrangement, as celestial as it is earthly. The witness of symphonic spirit makes sure that the fit exists and that it is vigorous on both sides of the relation ("absolute" spirit cares for the connectedness of *all* the sides). While hegemonic strands in Christian theology will aver that God is the absolute being-with subtending every relation, Hildegard is convinced—and here I am returning to a point I have made earlier—that the gathering place for spiritual gathering is Adam's voice before the Fall, his angelic voice "in which all the harmonies sounded and before which all the musical arts were to be found wanting [*in cuius voce sonus omnis harmonie et totius musice artis, antequam delinqueret*]" (*Epist.* XXIII, 100–101; CCCM 91, p. 64). Universal justice, fittingness, and adjustment were collected in a singular kind of being, the being that, despite being two, was one of a kind.

Things change after the Fall: instrumental music is a weak reverberation of prelapsarian harmonies. Devil's work, almost directly attributed by Hildegard to the prelates at Mainz, who issued an edict forbidding singing and playing of music in church liturgy, aggravates the situation from within. Why "from within"? Because this work neither introduces nor produces anything new; it only subverts symphonic resonances, by interfering with their reciprocal adjustments, so that "unjust oppressions [*iniustas depressiones*]" mount up (*Epist.* XXIII, 112–13; CCCM 91, p. 64).

Due to the progressively limited capacity of our voices to welcome and to resonate with the world, symphonic spirit migrates from one singular being receptive to universality to another, from the human to the plant. (Saints are exceptional in this respect: they are the most vegetal of humans. Consequently, addressing Rupert, a seventh-century saint, who was Bishop of Worms as well as of Salzburg, Hildegard says: "In you, the Holy Spirit symphonizes [*In te symphonizat Spiritus sanctus*]" [*Symph.* 49.5].) The greening green of *viriditas* supplants, or supplements, the symphonic structure of the soul in the same epistolary message to the prelates where Hildegard sketches out her theory of music. By stating that the soul enables and invigorates the body, she hints that the soul is the body's *viriditas*, that is, the self-refreshing power of the body, the power responsible for bodily renewal and regeneration, whether in itself (thanks to what we now call "cell division" and "tissue repair") or in another (by way of reproduction, sexual or asexual).

Crucially, *viriditas* is the power of the body exuded by corporeality without any external impositions. Understood in terms of *viriditas*, the soul is vegetal and *of the body*. It orchestrates the body's germination and blossoming, growth and metamorphosis. It moves the body, or spotlights the body's own capacity for self-movement, seeing that metamorphosis and growth cover half of what Aristotle considered as kinetic modalities. Finally, also apropos of Aristotle, the soul conceived as "the *viriditas* of the body" re-hashes, in a theoretical replay of *to threptikon*, the vegetal principle of vitality predicated on a two-pronged competence: nourishment and reproduction.

A definition of the soul through *viriditas* does not preclude the soul's symphonicity. Rejuvenating and maintaining the body, nutrition and reproduction are the most intimate of social processes, the physiologies of being-with. Throughout these processes, one is with the other, even if the other is already (or still) inside one, even if the other is still to come or no longer there. The nourishing resounds with and within the nourished; the generated vibrates with and within the generating . . . A good fit between the two terms in these relations must be ensured in every situation, such that, for instance, the nourishing is compatible with the digestive system of the nourished and the generating shares the blood type (or the rootstock) with the generated. Biological compatibility is a manifestation of ontological fittingness, of justice as the relational adjustment of the one to the other. The "correlations" of the nourishing and the nourished, of the generating and the generated, within the bounds of *viriditas* are symphonies of the body—of bodies articulated with one another in space, of the decaying body and its refreshed version (an articulation in time), of the old and of newness that springs from it in the perennial spring of the greening green.

The sequence of *viriditas* in Hildegard's symphonic justice extends past her epistolary writings. In *Scivias* she declares that she has known God "in works of justice [*te Deum meum in operibus iustitiae cognovero*]" (II.5.54; CCCM 43, p. 219). Actual fittingness, the work of attunement, has the effect of tuning the soul in to God. There is surplus work (perhaps, of an unintended variety) in works of justice, involving an adjustment of psychic life to the knowledge of the divine.

In the continuation of the passage from *Scivias* I have just cited, Hildegard adds another sign or site, through which and at which she comes to know God: "and I will know you in the *viriditas* of my soul [*in viriditate animae meae*]" (II.5.54; CCCM 43, p. 219). She establishes relations of equivalence between works of justice and *viriditas*, with both pointing the human soul toward an extraordinary cognition. To be precise, *viriditas* is not only "of my soul"; it *is* my soul as the self-refreshing power of the body. This power affects the body in the same way works of justice exert their influence on the world: they heal. Reinserting terms back in relational constellations, works of justice and *viriditas* bring things together into a resonant affinity. They give what is nearing its end a future. Stretching time out, binding its wounds, caring for the tears and intermittencies that make time what it is, they restage creation and lead the soul through the more or less circuitous routes to the creator. In a typically Augustinian gesture, Hildegard spots God not outside but in her core, in a momentary overcoming of temporal dispersion. Yet, this is an interiority that immediately turns inside out, inasmuch as it involves vegetal life and the actuality of just works in the world.

It is impossible to say with any degree of certainty where symphonic justice ends and *viriditas* begins. At their confluence, we find the fittingness of being to beings, the ever imperfect, perfectible, practical enabling of beings to continue to be, which nineteenth-century evolutionary thought reductively explained as "survival of the fittest." Symphonic justice and *viriditas* transcribe into quasi-musical and quasi-biological notations the tempos of existence, the rhythms of resonances that together constitute time. To exist is persistently to occupy oneself with acts of self-refreshing justice, to keep adjusting to existence, even if these acts are, at bottom, nothing but passive forbearance, *pathos*, patience: "that is how patience is learned [*patientiam sic discunt*]" (*Epist.* CCXXr, 119; CCCM 91A, p. 484). The duration of a life, its perdurance, is a stretch of patient endurance, the span in which the living is the stretching and the stretched.

One learns the art of patience in the face of the northern wind that causes all things to fail, trampling over "the sweet and useful herbs of virtue [*dulces et utiles herbas virtutum*]" (*Epist.* CCXXr, 117; CCCM 91A, p. 484). The analogy between good deeds and useful plants has surfaced in *Physica*. Resilient, the doers of such deeds cling to the work of justice, the major and minor injustices that disrupt their lives notwithstanding, "and so, aromatic vapors [*fumus aromatum*], which the angels breathe in, rise from their heart of hearts. With this, *viriditas* is granted to the good [*viriditas bonis tribuitur*]" (*Epist.* CCXXr, 123; CCCM 91A, p. 484). Being and being good are inextricably linked: before leaning one way or another, the soul is good insofar as it *is* and may continue in being, that is, insofar as it is symphonic and full of *viriditas*. The sensory dimension of this fullness matters. We have heard how the greening green of *viriditas* sounds. We have seen what it looks like, too. Now we can smell it in the whiff of aromatic herbs that evoke the rising vapors of spirit, warding off "the many ills of evil spirits" (*Physica* I; *PL* 197:1128), and growing on a terrain plowed by good deeds.

The synesthesia of *viriditas* in its audible and other sensory registers becomes richer still. Sounds resonate with sounds, with sights and smells, tactile impressions and flavors. When it comes to actual vegetation, synesthetic blends are plainly manifest. As Hildegard sings in "O Beloved Son," divinity "has arranged / in my entrails / all kinds of music in all the flowers of the tones [*in visceribus meis / omne genus musicorum / in omnibus floribus tonorum / constituit*]" (*Symph.* 71.5–10). Musical tonalities are flowers blossoming in the virgin flesh, blossoming *as* this flesh even in the dark of the body's entrails. They are heard-seen-smelled from within, immediately exposing visceral interiority to the outside, causing it to vibrate to divinely induced rhythms that are, simultaneously, its very own.

What philosophers dub "the synthetic unity of the object" in mental representation evinces a hidden vegetal-synesthetic source of our cognition. But, unlike the philosophical yardstick of clarity and distinctness, the experience of *viriditas* reaches us through a veil of tears and to the accompanying sounds of sighs and moans, blurring, muffling, and otherwise softening the sharp outlines of the perceived "object." "From these sighs and tears, penitent *viriditas* is recovered in every human [*de suspiriis et lacrimis istis viriditas penitentie in eodem homine exurgit*]" (*LDO* I.4.xxxii; *CCCM* 92, p. 168). In Letter 143, as well, the righteous who suffer from injustice cry out to God "groaning tearfully [*lacrimabili gemitu*]" before they are granted the gift of *viriditas* (*Epist.* CCXXr, 119; *CCCM* 91A, p. 484).

The visual and auditory accompaniment tears and groans provide is perversely symphonic, the lament resounding in and suitable to a broken, unjust reality eager to heal. Hildegard realizes with pained lucidity that her world (like that of Rupert and, to a still greater extent, ours) is a "shipwrecked world [*naufragus mundus*]" (*Symph*. 47.5). In contrast to Rupert who abandons it (*naufragum mundum / reliquisti*), and whom she does not rebuke for this desertion, she feels the urge to rescue and heal it. The symphonies of bodies, souls, things, modes of being resounding on the shipwreck that is the world would have been empty of substance were they simply to evoke a dream of paradisiac harmony. They carry with them, instead, a memory of suffering and draw their strength, empower the power of *viriditas*, from the present of sighs and tears.

Devastation yields fertile ground for the resurgence of the greening green. Surely, the outward signs of affliction distort the representations of objects. But the distortion is more accurate than clear sight and distinct hearing, since it gives the evidence of actual injustice and nonadjustment implanted into the order of things after the Fall. Vision and hearing are the breeding grounds of illusions, when they are without a veil of tears and a chorus of groans. That is also a movement in the grand symphony Hildegard is listening to, the symphony of damaged, mutilated, disarticulated, shipwrecked souls, bodies, and worlds.

In another letter, this time to the Archbishop of Bremen, dating from 1148, Hildegard commends the nun Richardis, the archbishop's sister, with words that mix vegetal imagery and musical terminology. "Now listen [*Nunc audi*]!" she appeals: Richardis is "like a flower blossoming with beauty and propriety in a symphony, through which the world appears [*velut flos in pulchritudine et decore in symphonia huius seculi appareret*]" (*Epist*. XIIIr, 12–13; CCCM 91, p. 30). A few lines below, she will tacitly compare Richardis to the Virgin Mary, changing her vegetal incarnation to "a virgin branch [*virginea virga*]" (*Epist*. XIIIr, 15; CCCM 91, p. 30). Whatever plant organ is more appropriate for the analogy, the underlying message is that the beauty of blossoming and flourishing is given not only to the eye but also to the ear; that its symphonic resonances let the world appear in the co-appearance of those who share it; that beauty is the symphony of the sonorous and the silent, the phonic and the aphonic. "Propriety," which Hildegard appends to beauty, stands for infinitely more than the chaste modesty of a virgin. It carries the connotations of appropriateness, of a fitting connection, of fittingness that adjusts each resonance to all the others and the whole to each one.

It follows that attempts, such as those rebuffed in Letter 23, to silence songs of praise or to drown out the vibrations of nonhuman (say, vegetal) beings meddle with symphonic justice. They interfere with the individual adjustments among sonorities as much as with the global fit of what resounds and the relative silence, from which resonance emerges and back to which it recedes. Those who "impose silence [*silentium imponunt*] on the church" are unjust; careless, they "open the closed and close the open [*claudenda aperiant et aperienda claudant*]" (*Epist.* XXIII, 147, 151; CCCM 91, p. 65). Worse, their interdiction blocks the openness of every finite opening, that is to say, of the world. The closure of the open, like the opening of the closed, rends the world by cutting its spatial and temporal connections: the articulations of those who share a world with one another and the resonances of their past and present or future versions. To impose silence is to efface altogether the faint boundaries between the voice and the one who emits and receives it, to let the void swallow up meaningful vibrations and covibrations of the vocal cords and musical instruments, plant leaves and roots, the soul and the body, the soul and other souls that, abiding in the voice, render it symphonic. It is to detain the creative divine finger (*digitus Dei*), which is the Holy Spirit (*Scivias* II.5.60; CCCM 43, p. 222) busy with bringing the world into being and playing its chords. (A memory evocative of the musicality of creation, of God striking the chords of the world, and with this act "worlding" it, is preserved in "instruments played with the flexing of the fingers" [*Epist.* XXIII, 98–101; CCCM 91, p. 64].)

In her era, Hildegard concludes, "the justice of God is weak [*iustitia Dei debilis est*]" (*Epist.* XXIII, 159; CCCM 91, p. 66). The symphony of existence is scarcely audible, the adjustments of each participant to the others and to the whole virtually nonexistent. Relational push and pull is feeble, and incongruence rules there where nothing fits anything at all. Hildegard calls this era "womanly times [*tempus muliebre*]" (*Epist.* XXIII, 158–59; CCCM 91, pp. 65–66), no doubt because the recipients of her letter unconsciously associate womanhood with weakness. But something does not add up here; something is incongruent with (and maladjusted to) the canvas Hildegard has painted so far.

"The" woman and flesh-and-blood women, from Mary to Richardis and Hildegard herself, are on the side of divine justice and vegetal life: attuned at once to the outside and the inside, they cherish mutual adjustment, fittingness, and relational *strength*. This would indicate that "the" woman is not a symptom of the epochal malaise, but a cure: when the justice of God is weak, women need to step in and step up to fortify it. "Womanly times" are also the times of the woman, the appropriate, good times for women to act. Hildegard confirms this exegetical trajectory in the following sentence: "When the strength of divine justice evaporates, a female warrior struggles with injustice, so that it may be defeated [*Sed fortitudo iustitie Dei exsudat, et bellatrix contra iniustitiam exsistit, quatenus devicta cadat*]" (*Epist.* XXIII, 159–61; CCCM 91, p. 66).

As a coda to this chapter, I want to revisit Hildegard's image of the body as the garment of the soul and, in the first place, her comment that it "has a living voice [*vivam vocem habet*]," fittingly—that is, justly—employed to "sing praises to God." (This already quoted thesis from Letter XXIII recurs in *Acta* [XI.165; *PL* 197:65b–c].) What interests me is not so much the soul's living voice *per se* as the having, or coming to have, one. It will be said, without further ado, that *having* manages the logic of appropriation: the soul is the proprietor of the body, which, as a result, acquires a living voice, is imbued with life by virtue of becoming the soul's possession. But property acquisition grants us extremely restricted access to the meaning of *having*. The semantic range of *habere* needs to be amplified for us to appreciate the full significance of "having a living voice."

Having a voice is, in Aristotelian terms, a disposition, a mere potentiality to break the silence, if only temporarily. To voice oneself is to act upon that potentiality, to exercise a capacity coextensive with one's body, to flesh it out in actual enunciations, songs, cries, groans, croaking, clicking, and the more delicate sound waves and vibrations. Silencing is freezing the passage from potentiality to actuality, so that the having (in this case, the having of a voice) turns into a vacuous possibility. Without the actuality of an act, the voice is no longer living. A plunge into silence ordained from above, as in the prohibition of certain liturgical elements by the prelates from Mainz, deadens the voice. Contrary to gnostic beliefs, the corporeal garment of the soul is anything but an expendable addition to the soul, to be cast off at the end of biological life as though it were a distraction from what really matters. In the absence of this clothing, the soul has no actuality, no effectual way of being in the world, no voice.

The silencing of plants leaves their voices at the level of a disposition, not even acknowledged as such. That they are incapable of acting, that they do not have or do not exercise their voices, and that their bodies/voices are hardly living—all these false assumptions belong together. The silence foisted on church services, as far as their musical components are concerned, robs the ecclesiastic voice of actuality, which expresses its "motherly" supplication for its children. So, in *Scivias*, the church is "the mother of the faithful [*mater fidelium*]," who "has a voice in sighing for her children [*gemebundam vocem in filiis suis habet*]" and who "has . . . this voice [*vocem habet*]" in order to advise God "to always see and think of [his] only-begotten incarnation . . . and, for the love of him, spare her children" (II.4.11; CCCM 43, p. 168). The voice of the church is that of a mediator, a messenger, an angelic presence that, on the one hand, sighs for its children and, on the other, counsels God. When it no longer has this voice, or when it has a voice that may not resound, its acts of mediation come to a grinding halt. A subtraction of being-with from sym-phonic spirit suffocates spirit itself. Imprisoning a voice in the silence of mere potentiality pillages the actuality of the body that it is and cuts the cord that holds it fast to life.

With the motherly figure of the church, the nonappropriative drift of "having a voice" is more pronounced. In potentiality and in actuality, the church has a voice for the other, sighing and singing for its children and for God. Forcing it into silence is separating it from alterity and jailing it in itself. Since the voice is the body, its confinement in itself is a body shut in itself: a corpse. Having a *living* voice is resonating with the other, for the other. If so, then plants have some of the most intensely living bodies/voices, reverberating with the elements, the seasons, and the planets, atmospheric phenomena and climates, other plants and animals. They have a voice, as well, in the sighing and singing of *viriditas* that permeates every form of life, painted in brilliant green. They have, make, and remake the world.

MISSIVES

This movement consists of an impossible combination of two completely different instruments, two souls, violoncello and piano. The piano with its short strokes and the cello with a play of possibilities. It is a fragmented game that seeks contact in the other without actually achieving it. The unattainable becomes a leading part in itself.

5 mins 20 secs

~~

Missives

Throughout her life, Hildegard maintained copious correspondence with popes and monarchs, prelates, abbots and abbesses, nuns and monks. The most consequential of these is the letter she addressed to Bernard, Abbot of Clairvaux, in 1146–47, beseeching him to support her work in the name "of the highest Father, who has sent the Word with sweet *viriditas* into the womb of the Virgin [*per altitudinem Patris, qui in suavi viriditate misit Verbum in Virginis uterum*]" (*Epist.* I, 53–54; CCCM 91, p. 5). More than thirty years later, in the 1179 letter to Christian, Archbishop of Mainz, Hildegard will repeat roughly the same formulation, writing that "the eternal Father, in sweet *viriditas*, sent his Word into the womb of the Virgin for the salvation of humanity [*eterni Patris . . . pro salute hominis in suavi viriditate misit Verbum suum in Virginis uterum*]" (*Epist.* XXIV, 64–65; CCCM 91, p. 68).

Like musical flowers arranged in virgin entrails, the recurring summons of a flourishing womb, within which the creative Word blossoms, alludes to the miraculous expression of God that is the incarnation. If the Word accompanying *viriditas* is clothed with flesh in the Virgin, then that flesh is not just theandric, but phytotheandric: vegetal-divine-human. The Word speaks out of the womb, delivering its message of salvation from there. Not necessarily vocalizing, verbalizing, or communicating anything, it flowers. (Vocalization, verbalization, and communication should not, under any circumstances, be conflated with expression.) In the Virgin, out of the Virgin, the Word bound up with the greening green speaks wordlessly, by engendering the One who would redeem the world, refresh and rejuvenate it, once the world's own quantum of self-rejuvenating power had critically dwindled. The Word is, therefore, expressed in the language of plants (of flowers, even), and it merges with the vibrant silence that enables speech.

In both epistolary enunciations, the Word is situated, swathed, encased in *viriditas*, as though *viriditas* were a gift-wrapping, in which it was sent. Is *viriditas* superficial, as well as all-encompassing, with respect to the Word? Is it but the outer envelope for the evangelical message? Or the material form, in which and as which this message is received? Be this as it may, the preponderance of *viriditas* over the Word, sent with and in it, is not at all domineering. The greening green receives the divine missive prior to Mary, who, herself full of *viriditas*, will have taken over the reception. At its final destination, the Word arrives in a virgin womb, the womb on a vegetal-divine-human verge. Thereafter, Mary will contribute to shaping that which, or the One whom, is so received, relaying the vegetal and divine dimensions and adding a human aspect to him. She will indicate that reception is an act that is beyond activity and passivity: receiving the Word already received by *viriditas*, the mother-matter of the salvific figure also transforms it. What the sending signifies can only be appreciated through reckoning with this maternal, material, matriarchal, or matri-anarchal welcome.

Hildegard locates Christ in the middle between his divine send-off and return to God in vegetal flesh. A pertinent passage from *Scivias* is worth citing at length, considering that it encapsulates the overall movement of sending in Hildegard's reading of the scriptures. "The Father testifies that before the ages he begot his one fruitful Word [*unicum fructuosum Verbum*], through which all things were made; and then, at the appointed time, the Word gloriously flowered in the Virgin [*in praedestinato tempore in Virgine gloriosissime florui*]. The Word testifies that he went forth [*exivit*] from the Father and inclined himself toward human nature, becoming incarnate in the purity of virginity. He went forth from the Father a spirit and returned again to the Father in fruitful flesh [*in carnis fructuositate*]; and so he stands in the middle [*in medio positum*], since he was invisibly begotten by the Father before time began, and conceived in the body within time by the Holy Spirit in the womb of the Virgin" (*Scivias* III.7.8; CCCM 43, p. 472).

We will have a chance to pore over the details of the divine sending, that is, over the comings and goings of the Word. Note, for now, that the testimonies vary according to the speakers who give them. The perspective of the sender is different from that of the sent; the Father and the Word narrate distinct aspects of the same process. The former outlines the origins of the Word and its arrival at the destination; the latter describes its egression from the source and inclination toward humanity. God the Father touches upon the beginning and the end, as well as on what happened before the beginning, prior to the order of time; the incarnate Word describes the middle, while contemplating the meaning of being in the middle. In the portion of the text I have not included in the quotation, the Holy Spirit gives us access to what we might call "the beginning of the middle," the conditions of possibility for the Word's reception in Mary, whom it "enkindled [*accendit*]." Only a Trinitarian vision is capable of combining various perspectives in a "heavenly testimony [*caeleste testimonium*]" (*Scivias* III.7.8; CCCM 43, p. 472) that incorporates these points of view into a vision of the One in plurality and of plurality in the One.

Although the Virgin Mary herself does not bear witness to the sending on the side of its reception, her outlook is glistening between the lines and in the cracks and fissures crisscrossing the narratives that constitute a divine phenomenology. Within the version of events narrated by God the Father, her reception of the Word scrambles the usual order of temporal succession, as marked by the stages of vegetal growth and reproduction: the fruitful Word (*fructuosum Verbum*) flowered (*florui*) in her. The "appointed time" of the Word's descent into the world evinces theological seasonality, a blossoming or a coming to fruition at just the right moment, in an upshot of divine justice. Yet, its glorious, shining, flowering appearance in Mary sends shock waves through the time of the seasons that, according to the rules of "verginity" I've sketched earlier, begins moving countercurrent-wise, from fruit back to the flower. In due time, the course of time drastically changes to the point of being revolutionized—not in the instant of the Word's sending, but at the stage of its reception.

Mary's silent testimony speaks through the words of the Word, too. Drawing near her, the Word is inclined toward human nature (*inclinans se ad humanam naturam*), which means that she, toward whom the Word inclines itself, stands for this very nature. The human is said in the feminine here. Thanks to being in her, by virtue of blossoming out of her, the Word incarnate as Christ becomes phytotheandric. Tilting, leaning, bending down to "the purity of [her] virginity," to virgin uprightness that puts her in the neighborhood of virility, the Word sent by God is received in a manner not factored into the sending. By the time it arrives, so inclined, it loses *its* straightness, the straightforwardness of pure spirit. The entire temporal order, the body, flowering flesh, femininity, and virginity are so many unavoidable digressions, diversions, detours on the itinerary of the divine missive that make it what it finally must become without the end transparently visible from the beginning.

From the standpoint of God the Father, the dispatch completes a perfect circle, begotten as a fruitful Word and returning to the progenitor in fruitful flesh. Nonetheless, it is the middling position (*in medio positum*: which is not at all a position but a way of moving with all its serendipitous divagations, adventitious offshoots, and eventful encounters) that matters from the perspective of the incarnate Son. The middle of the sending, itself said in the middle voice, is its vegetal moment *par excellence*, brimming with attention to the milieu wherein it takes place, to hybridizations and cross-pollinations, to growth as a striving toward the other or others, to the "meanwhile," the *in medias res*, out of which the fabric of time is knit. Spatiotemporally intermediate, bracketed by its *genesis* and *eschaton*, the world is the place and time in-between, which hints at the fact that it is always a world of plants.

Jesus's utterance, as Hildegard relays it, "my Father has sent me into the world, so that I would save it [*pater meus ad hoc me misit in mundum, ut salvum faciam illum*]" (*LDO* II.1.xliv; CCCM 92, p. 334), insinuates that he has been sent into the middle of existence in order to save the middle, the interval and interspace that is the world. Since his first milieu is the Virgin Mary's womb, in which he will have blossomed, the world that is to be saved, just like the Savior himself, is vegetal from beginning to end—hence, without either beginning or end, in a relentless middle. His mission, then, is saving the vegetal in the human, the human in the vegetal, the vegetal in the vegetal, the world in the world.

God's sending of the fruitful Word into the world finds a humble and tacit, albeit self-conscious, reflection in Hildegard's epistolary activity. So, writing to Pope Eugenius in 1148, she implores: "Prepare this writing for the hearing of those who receive me and make it *viridem* with the juice of sweet flavor [*et fac illam viridem in suco suavis gustus*]; make it a root of the branches and a leaf flying into the face of the devil [*et radicem ramorum et volans folium contra diabolum*], and you will have eternal life" (*Epist.* II, 24–26; CCCM 91, p. 8). Preparations for the reception of writing are carried out in the middle between its sending and its arrival at the destination. That is where it bristles with *viriditas*, recalling the greening green of the Word sent into the Virgin Mary's womb. It could well be that writing's reception is but an extension of these preparations, from which it issues and cannot be entirely dissociated. What is certain is that, in the preparatory middle, writing is vegetalized beyond a formal analogy with the *viriditas* of the divine missive.

As she prepares her writing for a proper reception, Hildegard entrusts it to different parts of plants: roots and branches, fruity juice and leaves. There are two main methods of sending that orient these provisions: sending-to and sending-against. Sent to those prepared to listen to its vibrant silence, the writing is distilled in the sweet essence of juice (*sucus*), in which, according to the argument of *Physica*, the earth itself is distilled and purified, and which exemplifies the inherence of the soul in the body. Still in its positive mode, the missive is akin to the branches of a root, a sending forth that does not radically depart from its point of emission but grows ever more complex, ramified, overarching and overhanging. That root is rooted elsewhere, notably in "true light [*verum lumen*]."

Sent against the devil—Hildegard's shorthand for a force opposed to the power of *viriditas*—the writing detaches from its source and the folio is converted into a *folium*, a page into a leaf. As in the flowering of the fruitful Word upon contact with Mary, time flows back in this conversion, resurrecting the plant at the material source of a piece of paper. That is the second feat the ephemeral leaf, no longer connected to the tree on which it flourished, accomplishes. The first is the act of detachment, of letting go, of strength educed from apparent weakness.

The leaf that is Hildegard's writing, sent against the devil and against the blockages of *viriditas* that are the devil's negative doing, puts itself at the mercy of air and wind, of unpredictable atmospheric pathways that would guide it in the right direction. Yet, despite the illusion of a chance release, to let go of writing is not to throw it out haphazardly and at a random moment: the throw requires as much preparation as the sending of branches from the root for the sake of "those who receive me." No dissemination without insemination; no meaningful detachment without attachment to the root, which also grows, moves, changes, develops, gathers a cross-species community around itself.

In a prophetic fashion, Hildegard explains in a missive addressed to Eberhard, Bishop of Bamberg, that her words are not really hers: "I am but a poor woman, looking out into true light, in which I have seen and heard the true vision of what I am expounding before you. And this exposition does not consist of my words, but of true light, which has no defects and which I hereby transmit [*ita expositum non verbis meis, sed veri luminis, cui numquam ullus defectus est, in hunc modum transmitto*]" (*Epist.* XXXIr, 9–11; CCCM 91, p. 83). A mediator, if not the medium where the luminous message travels, Hildegard situates herself in the middling position she shares with plants and with the incarnate Word. Her angelic words (which are avowedly not hers: *non verbis meis*) impart the Word sent into the world, into this constitutively finite time-place wedged between the beginning and the end. Between sending and receiving, at once receiving and sending the light of meaning, she fosters the becoming of the world, the world's becoming-world, the becoming of becoming. As a root, she is at the same time a branch, carrying light in an objectified, written form, from the radiant source to its multiple, ramified destinations.

Similarly claiming that she is a "poor little woman" in a letter to Pope Eugenius, Hildegard spells out the reception and sending of the "living light" scintillating in her words. "You have seen some of my writings of true visions," she writes, "which I received from the living light [*vivens lux*], and you have listened to these visions in the embraces of your heart . . . But still the same light has not left me [*eadem lux non reliquit me*] . . . Therefore, I sent this letter to you now as God has instructed me. And my soul desires that the light of light shine in you [*lumen de lumine in te luceat*] and purify your eyes and arouse your spirit to the work of these writings [*et spiritum tuum exsuscitet ad opus scripture istius*] (*Epist.* II, 5–11; CCCM 91, pp. 7–8). The living light passes through Hildegard's writings to the eyes and hearts of others without abandoning her altogether. Its staying power in her soul is not commensurate with stagnation; the light remains with her, rooted in her yet also deriving from beyond her, so as to move on and shine elsewhere, to keep working, to continue putting her writings to work (*ad opus*). It stays in order to renew the sending, to grow, to resend it again and again as fresh branches, flowers, and leaves. That is why the light is living: the resumption of its transmissions is due to the power of the greening green pulsing in it.

Nel mezzo del cammin di nostra vita, "in the middle of our life's journey": this is the beginning—the very first verse—of the *Divine Comedy*. Dante's masterpiece begins in the middle, from the middle of a life, and, in doing so, indicates that life itself begins in the middle, much like a thought, a new sentence, or a germinating seed. Life is split into an infinity of transmission lines, extending between its sending and reception, the wandering, divergent, irregular, jagged lines that meet on the horizons of vitality.

Hildegard couches her thoughts on the immanence of life, always already located in the middle of life, in a letter to the Bishop of Bamberg. She writes there: "But life is in life. A tree flourishes from nothing else but *viriditas*, and even a stone is not without moisture, nor is any other creature without its power. For eternity itself is alive and not without floridity [*Sed vita est in vita. Arbor enim non floret, nisi de viriditate, nec lapis est sine humore, nec ulla creatura sine vi sua. Ipsa etiam vivens eternitas non est sine floriditate*]" (*Epist.* XXXIr, 18–21; CCCM 91, p. 83). "Life is in life": this eccentric state of being-in makes it alive. Life is, therefore, immersed, swathed, or sheathed in itself, though "in itself" as completely other to itself. A tree is a living being that is in life as a result of *viriditas* permeating it; a stone is a form of life that is in life signaled by moisture; the life, in which every creature is, designates that entity's own power, which is at the same time distinct from it and which, much later, Spinoza will grasp as *conatus essendi*.

Completing the list of the folds of immanence is a living eternity, *vivens aeternitas*, a life that is in life thanks to its floridity, the flowering creative of countless modes of existence. *Floriditas* is, without a doubt, a grammatical and logical counterpart of *viriditas*. It is the flourishing that, most conspicuous in plants, is shared by all forms of life. Nevertheless, the parallel comes to an end once the fullness of actuality, in which *floriditas* abides, frees it from the potency, potentiality, and power implied in the root *vir*. *Floriditas* is ineffably strong in its presumed weakness, as is the generative but nonproductive virginity of Mary, whose "floridity / God foresaw on the first day / of his creation [*floriditatem tuam / Deus in prima die / creature sue previderat*]" (*Symph.* 20.3a). No wonder that Hildegard prefaces it with a double negative ("is not without floridity," *non est sine floriditate*), following the *via negativa* of mystical knowledge shorn of direct access to divine attributes, such as a living eternity.

The middle is what is most alive in a life: it is what enlivens the fringes and extreme edges that are, likewise, in the middle, no matter how remote from the "midpoint." Hildegard's expression *vita est in vita* accentuates the spatiality of the vital nucleus, which is equally temporal as *the meantime* of living, the interim of being alive, even at the end of a life. The reduplication of the substantive *vita* buries the time of the middle as effectively as the middle voice of "living" (as, for example, in *vivens aeternitas*) unearths it. Behind the façade of substantivization, life addresses and sends itself to life in the course of living; life receives in itself a life that is being lived. Living beings are its messages and messengers, all of them angelic, intermediate, interlaced with one another and with life, from which, in which, and to which they are launched.

꙳

The inwardness of life calls for further elaboration—not only with an eye to the existential take on being-in (being alive as being in life) that, as Heidegger explains in *Being and Time*, is worlds apart from water poured into a glass, but also keeping in mind the multiple turns and twists of this interiority. If "life is in life," then it is inside and outside, outside in and inside out. While fully immanent, folded into itself, life is ecstatically beside itself, like a soul that, having discovered God in its core, is thrown into the world by its divine indwelling. The "in" of life wrapped in life is that of the in-between and, especially, of the edges between interiority and exteriority. Without these edges, absent their interruptions and discontinuities, no sending is possible and no reception, because there is no distance, no respite, no time-space to stretch the transmission lines of vitality relaying nothing but themselves.

Assuming that the inwardness of life is predicated on its being in-between, the dwelling it provides is inherently open and accommodating to the outside. In human existence, one kind of life is appropriate to welcoming divinity, and that is the life of justice: "Only humans living justly are the tabernacle of God, for God dwells in them [*Nam quidem homines iuste viventes tabernaculum Dei sunt, quia Deus in eis habitat*]" (*Epist.* XLVr, 9–10; CCCM 91, p. 114). A just life is in life in such a manner that it is adjusted to the living, attuned to various intersecting and, at times, clashing transmission lines of vitality. Or, better, it is in the process of patiently and continuously adjust*ing* to life, spanning (unreconciled) the life within and the life without. It is the exemplary in-between. The tautological doubling of the line from Hildegard's text, divided in half by "for" (*quia*) is, in this sense, necessary to complete the structure of outer and inner vitalities, of a life that is nestled in life.

In the same 1173 letter to Conrad, Bishop of Worms, Hildegard nevertheless widens the circle of divine indwelling from those leading a just life to all humans: "A human is the edifice of God, in which he dwells because he sent the fiery soul into it, the soul that flies with rationality in expansion, just as a wall encompasses the breadth of a house [*Homo enim edificium Dei est, in quo ipse mansionem habet, quoniam igneam animam in illum misit, que cum rationalitate in dilatatione volat, quemadmodum murus latitudinem domus comprehendit*]" (*Epist.* XLV, 10–13; CCCM 91, p. 114). As in the previous sentence, the dwelling and the indwelt symmetrically replicate one another following the words *in quo ipse*, in order to attest to life that is in life. Now, however, the premise behind Hildegard's enlargement of God's dwelling, scaled up from a just life to any sort of human life, is that, in principle (or *in potentia*—according to its innate way of receiving the power of *viriditas*), humanity is a life attuned to lives, sent as a medium allowing for a better resonance of other vital media and messages. A goal to be achieved more than a species or a fixed kind of being, humanity does not consist only in doing justice and practicing the art of adjustment; it *is* adjustment and justice, an incarnation of the in-between, which it frequently betrays, thereby betraying itself.

God dwells in the human soul by virtue of a certain missive, if not a blazing missile he has sent (*misit*) there: fire. The house of God is a house on fire. Heat and light, transformation and preservation, spirit and matter converge in the image of a living dwelling evocative of a hearth, around which a house acquires its quality of habitability. We will get back to igneous things in the next chapter. What is of the essence in this letter is the sending of fire into a human soul that it fuels, powers, animates, and, in a way, ensouls.

Consider the sending itself on a par with the sent that prevents the soul from stagnating: the sending sends the soul that receives it upward; what is sent (fire) at once propels and dilates the soaring soul, conjuring up the image of a hot-air balloon. The dilating sphere is that of rationality, which is to say, of relationality. This means that the flight of an expanding rationality enriches the soul's relationality, impels it toward others, ever closer to the in-between time-space of an open dwelling.

Another hermeneutical door is left ajar in the passage from the letter to Conrad, and it leads us straight to Hildegard's ecology. On the one hand, the human soul is God's dwelling (*aedificium, mansio, domus*: all these are the terms of building, habitation, abiding) reconstructing the Greek *oikos* in Christianity. On the other hand, the principle and practice of rationality, that is to say of *logos*, is *how* God dwells there. Jointly, they amount to an ecology that the divine indwelling of the human irradiates outward to other forms of existence.

So construed, Hildegard's theanthropocentrism is fresh and refreshing, strengthening the transmission lines that run from life to life, suffused with the greening green. It launches us into the world, where ecology and humanity are the missions, far in excess of religious missionary activity, of helping the world become world, developing the relations out of which it is quilted, and allowing the human to become human as a result. There is no denying that, on the whole, humanity fails to receive this missive and betrays its mission in the course of a history, in which it does not become itself. Still, the actual debacle, the debacle that is our actuality, does very little to invalidate the steering of the soul toward a distinctly human "shape"—the in-between.

Sent into the body, every soul is a messiah, anointed to deliver the world, to free it to and for itself, to let it become (a world). The dispatches multiply, too: the sending of divine fire into the soul reflects and is infinitely reflected in the sending of the soul into the body. In addition, "all the arts that are useful and necessarily pertain to the human have been created by the breath, which God sent into the human body [*a spiraculo, quod Deus misit in corpus hominis, repertae sunt*]" (*Epist.* XXIII, 134–37; CCCM 91, p. 65). Fire is tossed together with breath, the oxygen required for its burning. At the material base of spirit is respiration that involves breathing with one's lungs and, in a more vegetal key, at the surface of one's body, through the pores of the skin. The breath of life God has destined for the human is external and internal, superficial and deep, intensive and extensional. It circulates in the intermediate region, which turns out to be airier, roomier, more capacious, with every inspiration and expiration, expanding without colonizing anything like the hot-air balloon of the soul itself.

The inspired body expires what has been sent its way creatively, propagating the life-giving impulse. Though foundational, divine inspiration does not linger inside the human, who gives it off in the form of art—of all the arts (*omnes artes*) that are useful—instead. And so, faltering, halting, a chain of transmissions continues. The refreshing power of *viriditas* steps in between each expiration and inspiration, where fire passes into air and air into fire.

ARDENCIES

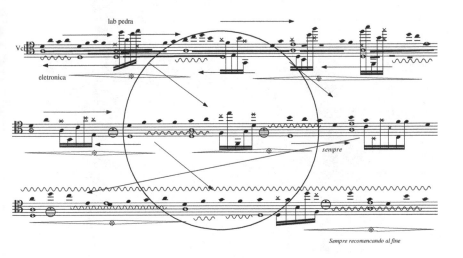

The leading voice, a cello, plays in the present and in a recent past, with an insistence on the task of keeping and preserving Hildegard's melodies. It is an intense cello that meets elements of a different kind. Stones seeking light and a threatening earth are mixed with an understanding of space. The wear and tear and the contradictions seek their mediations. The sentence ends with a chord in space that answers with a "perhaps."

6 mins 33 secs

Ardencies

EVERYTHING IS A PLAY OF FIRE, which is itself an interplay of the two powers, the two potentialities we have already encountered in this book: light and heat, illumination and ardor, accessible through visual and tactile impressions. This play and this interplay are as dangerous as they are indispensable for existence. Warmth is life-giving, while extreme heat may be life-depriving; intense light blinds and darkness does, too; light without heat is sterile, heat without light—all-consuming. The ecological and theological standoff, the *dead heat* of *viriditas* and *ariditas* pivots on the degrees of fire: on whether it is just right, too much, or too little to sustain life in the physical and spiritual senses Hildegard merges into a physico-spiritual sense.

When you get right down to it, *ariditas* has never been "only" a metaphor. It hastens global warming, which, in a circular fashion, expresses it, lending it a climatic body. Dry, scorching, deadening heat wells up as a result of persistent violations suffered by *viriditas* and the vegetal mediations, or modifications, of solar fire that refresh existence. Deforestation, desertification, *ariditas* as the negation of *viriditas* (or, more chillingly, as its negative manifestation in devastation that waxes creative, particularly compared to destruction)—these are the vicious and menacing repercussions of playing with fire, of the play and interplay of fire.

From the standpoint of Hildegard's pyrology, global warming is concurrent with a certain global cooling, with entropy, the dissipation of spirit's warmth, its seepage out of the world. In the third vision recorded in *Scivias*, the globe floats on the heat released by a sparkling flame raging under it. "And the globe at times raised itself up so that much fire flew to it [*et idem globus se aliquando sursum elevavit et plurimus ignis ei occurrit*], and thereby its flames lasted longer; and sometimes it sank downward and great cold [*multumque frigus*] came over it" (I.3; CCCM 43, p. 40). In terms of both its causes and its effects, the extreme heat of *ariditas* coincides with the frigid dearth of spirit, the world no longer in touch with itself at the height of its globalizing "integration." The rises and the falls of the globe, reflecting on a grand scale the rises and falls of a soul inspired by fire, are the physical movements that attest to fluctuations in the globe's properly spiritual connection to the divine and that *are* that very connection. That the mass of the globe does not mechanically fall but undergoes a series of ascents and descents evinces a surplus, engrained into physical reality, over physics and its laws. Spirit is this surplus over nature in nature, by means of which nature relates to itself. When one loses sight of the spiritual surplus, entropy is the sole conceivable future. The intolerable heat of global warming accords with global cooling.

God's manifestation in and as fire is a staple theme in Judaism and Christianity, and it is ubiquitous in Hildegard's writings. Turned up to the highest potency, the fire of God remains judicious and discerning beyond the limits of discernment we tend to associate with human understanding. So, "God consumes by the fire of his vengeance [*per ignem ultionis suae exurens*] all those who are outside the true faith, and those within the Catholic faith he purifies by the fire of his consolation [*per ignem consolationis*

suae purificat]" (*Scivias* I.3.3; CCCM 43, p. 42). The light of divine judgment accompanies the heat that, minutely adjusted to each singular case, either flares up and burns or purifies and consoles. The culmination of the two powers' union is the figure of Christ—"the sun of justice [*sol iustitiae*]," "with the brilliance of burning love [*fulgorem ardentis caritatis*], of such great glory that every creature is illuminated by the brightness of his light" (*Scivias* I.3.3; CCCM 43, p. 43).

Hildegard shares these suppositions and conclusions with the tradition. What is, I claim, unique to her vision is a tendency to moderate the brilliance and glory of fiery divinity with darkness and shadows. Here again, she does not swerve far from the central theme of Christian mysticism, going back to the beginnings of apophatic theology in Pseudo-Dionysius and, perhaps more cataphatically, to Augustine with his interior God, or forward to Meister Eckhart's nothingness and John of the Cross with his "dark nights." In congruence with a mystical fascination with darkness, Hildegard pinpoints, in the vision I have been consulting on these pages, a "dark fire [*tenebrosus ignis*]" (*Scivias* I.3; CCCM 43, p. 40), underlying the uneven flame responsible for the rises and falls of the globe, the peaks and valleys of spiritual history. She admits that tenebrous fire provoked such a feeling of horror (*tanti horroris*) in her that she could not look at it. Dark fire absorbs into itself the power of vision and the gaze, for which it remains impenetrable. Averting one's eyes from it is probably the last desperate attempt to reestablish control in the face of its implacable force.

Hildegard's construal of her emotional response as a reaction to the vilest acts of the devil embodied in dark fire falls short of convincing, though. Below the flame supporting the globe, the position of *tenebrosus ignis*, which burns but sheds no light, hints at how it may be more fundamental still than the world's igneous—brilliant and hot—spiritual foundations. An obscure disaster may happen at any moment; indeed, it has already happened in times immemorial and is simply prevented from breaking through by the fire of spirit interposed between it and the world. The globe's lowering brings the world closer to that ever present disaster, a horrible trauma at the zero point of creation.

Nevertheless, dark fire is not Hildegard's preferred vehicle for moderating the brilliance and glory of divine flames. Her mysticism is that of darkness, not of Darkness. She does not shy away from the shadows that, dancing with the light, put into relief or highlight the play of fire, its interplay with itself. Together, the luminosity of shadows and the obscurity of radiance bring about a living and enlivening light and warmth in an ecological twist on the theological tradition. They shape vegetal mysticism, where the mystery is etched right on the surface of the changing appearances.

In a revolutionary rotation, turning, once again, inside out, Mary's womb becomes a source of light, beaming from its blossom: "and your womb / illuminated all creatures / with the beautiful flower [*et venter tuus / omnes creaturas illuminavit / in pulcro flore*]" (*Symph.* 18.5–8). From a dark space of bodily interiority, the virgin womb passes into a place of luminosity, in part because the other power of fire it belongs with is not the heat of fallen desire but divine warmth. As Hildegard formulates it in another hymn: "God delighted in you / when he set within you / the embrace of his warmth [*cum aplexionem caloris sui*]" (*Symph.* 17.4, 2–5). But what is "within you" is actually outside; the inside has never been inside; you are outside yourself. There is no deep interiority in Mary's vegetal constitution, which is why her womb, fully exposed, can blossom.

Centuries later, Goethe will espy in flowers the objectifications of light, their diverse colors falling at different points of the light spectrum. Flowering is the expression of spirit in matter, the journey of a perpetually modified, metamorphosing leaf from the dense darkness of the soil, from which it never really separates, toward the sun and the air. For Hildegard, Christ the Flower is light *prior*

to its objectification; in him or through him, she spots the renais-
sance of light, a rebirth of the first light that shone at the creation
of the world. "O, Lady Savior," she exclaims, "you, who bore a
new light / for humankind [*Unde, o Salvatrix, / que novum lumen
/ humano generi protulisti*]" (*Symph.* 20.6b). The lighting up of
the world thanks to this event in the history of spirit complements
the rising of the globe due to an increase in the heat of subtending
fire, likewise attributed to the birth of Jesus. The event, for which
fire serves as a catalyst, does not come to a crescendo in blinding
celestial glow; it grows into a plant.

The flower that accommodates the two powers of fire manages
to reverse the phenomena of vegetal nature. We have already seen
how the verticality of plants is flipped, in a way reminiscent of Plato,
when the root is tethered to the sun and how, in a countercurrent
to plant becoming and the time of the seasons, Mary and Jesus leap
from the fruit back to the flower. Now, the same plant part turns
back the process of photosynthesis inasmuch as it is the source of
light and heat, as opposed to their recipient. The flower outshines
the sun. This movement against nature in nature is the movement
of spirit and, at the same time, of an ecological theology.

We would commit a grave error if we were to assume that the
event of Christ's birth is that of matter's spiritualization and that,
therefore, human-vegetal-divine *mater-materia* is in itself obscure
until it is clarified by the flower it births. We've heard Hildegard
calling Mary *lucida materia*, or luminous matter, a characterization
she confirms by invoking the Virgin's "brightness [*claritas*]": "the
supreme Father / took note of the Virgin's brightness [*supernus
Pater claritatem Virginis / atendit*]" (*Symph.* 21.17–18). In Jesus,
her *claritas* takes the form of a flower, described as "marvelously
bright [*mirabiliter clarus flos*]" (21.14). It is brightness vegetalized, nourished and nourishing together with warmth in the unity
of fire's dual power.

What does it mean for brightness to be vegetal, floral even? At
the very least, that it is not absolute, not absolved from its relation

with shadows and murkiness. Vegetal brightness is finite, despite its divine provenance. A living light is not just light, as it mingles with cool umbrage and with warmth. Spiritual matter is shot through with clarity; a living light is stitched of "luminous shadows [*lucida umbra*]" (*Symph.* 31.5). Indeed, luminous shadows are a privileged observation spot for the patriarchs and the prophets to behold "a keen and living light / budding on a branch / that blossomed alone / from the entrance of light taking root [*acutam et viventem lucem / in virga germinantem, / que sola floruit / de introit radicantis luminis*]" (31.6–9). Sheer plant immanence: from a vegetal site of luminous shadows, the prophets and the patriarchs, analogized to roots, are perceiving the glow of Christ the Flower on Mary the Branch. The soil and the root are illuminated, the shadows are luminous, but they keep a smattering of obscurity— their shadowiness—required for plants to grow and growing with the plants themselves. (The same holds, *mutatis mutandis*, for the "happy roots" planted in the "translucent shadow [*perspicue umbre*]" [32.5].)

The opposite of living light is a light that is either dead or deadening, scorching. Although the walls of Jerusalem "gleam with living stones [*muri tui / fulminant vivis lapidis*]" (49.8), the city's "foundations are made with scorching stones [*fundamentum tuum positum est / cum torrentibus lapidibus*]" (49.7). Hinting at Hildegard's take on the relation of Judaism and Christianity, the inorganic foundations of the celestial city breathe with unendurable heat, while the walls erected upon them grow plantlike with stones that are alive. The light of Jerusalem, too, parts ways with luminous shadows and vegetal brightness; a "light never darkened [*lux numquam obscurata*]" (49.1b), it floods from the metaphysical abyss between matter and spirit, between dark density and transparent luminosity. Translated into the language of fire, metaphysics builds itself up on a distinction between inorganic (unbridled, potentially unlimited) heat and light, on the one hand, and the reception of these signature powers of fire within the limits that circumscribe a life, on the other. For a "light never darkened," matter and mother, the one as the other (and both vegetalized in Aristotle's *hylé*, as well as in the Latin-derived *madera* or *madeira*, the woods or wood, mutating into "the greenest branch"), are darkness never lit. In the sphere of "luminous matter," vegetality is spirit, in which the moist freshness of *viriditas* is mixed with the slowly burning fire of life. Jerusalem is split down the middle between these metaphysical and nonmetaphysical constructions of its stones.

ᕔ

Hildegard posits semantic equivalence in saying that Mary's womb lights up and that the greenest branch blossoms with the flower of redemption. This is not "flowery" language, poetically inspired religious rhetoric divorced from reality, but a visionary (in all the senses of the word) braid, where fire and vegetality intertwine. In *Scivias*, Hildegard sums up the burning, bright, illuminated, lucid nature of Mary when she notes that her virginity was "glorious [*gloriosa*]." The scriptural attribute of God's glory is fire, adverting to Mary's divinization. In the field of Hildegard's vision, this process occurs *via vegetativa*: "so that when the Son of God too in virginal chastity showed marvelous splendor [*mirificum fulgorem*] and rendered virginity fecund [*fecunda virginitate*], virginity became glorious [*virginitas gloriosa effecta est*]" (*Scivias* I.3.5; CCCM 43, p. 44). The fecundity of virginity is indicated by the bright flower growing/glowing on the greenest branch, by Jesus's splendor (better: his glare, *fulgor*) that expresses, rather than ushers in, the flaming existence of Mary. Glory is the effect of that expression. The branch is aglow, and the flower is only a belated confirmation of its brightness. What or who is this matter or mother, wood and the woods, on fire?

"Fiery" is how Hildegard qualifies spirit, for instance in a hymn: "*O ignee Spiritus, laus tibi sit* [O fiery Spirit, praise to you]" (*Symph.* 27.1). To say that a branch and a flower are fiery is to spiritualize matter, the woods and wood burning without being reduced to ashes. The biblical story of the burning bush—one of God's apparitions before Moses—shimmers in a different light and exudes another kind of heat than the conflagration of metaphysical indestructibility. If the blaze is the burning of the bush itself, without a match taken to it; if this flame is what makes it green and full of life, then spirit as fire is in matter, and it is matter. The branch and its flower are on fire, because they *are* fire. The burning bush is suitable for a divine apparition for the same reason that virginal brightness welcomes "the entrance of light taking root": in their materiality, they are *of spirit*, which they receive into themselves as something *of themselves.*

On Hildegard's reading, the burning bush signifies a vegetal reconciliation of the one and the many, which is also that of matter and spirit. Or, more accurately, not their reconciliation but their fecund indeterminacy, their immediate and interminable passage into one another. "The great flock [*Turba magna*], which the burning bush / (seen by Moses) signifies, / is the flock God planted in the primal root [*quam Deus in prima radice plantaverat*] / in the human he formed out of clay / to live without commingling with men" (*Symph.* 65.9). Human multitude ("the great flock," a throng, a mob—*turba*) is immediately the one (Adam) initially made to live without the company of others like him. The root is the many, who are there right from the beginning, or maybe before and without a beginning, anarchically, in the one. Today, plant scientists invoke the "swarm intelligence" of plant roots, decentralized, with innumerable points of contact, communication, and decision making. The very first human is, according to Hildegard, a swarm without a center, the many in the one generated at the extreme as separate, autistic, incommunicable, meant initially to lead the kind of existence that does not involve a "commingling with men" but that is not exempted from a "great flock of life" within. This root, which grows into a bush, is burning; however, it does not burn up because it is many—that is, because, infinite in its finitude, it has no definite outlines of the one who (or that) may be wiped out, expended, or otherwise destroyed as a unified whole.

Fire and the heat it releases generally respond to this ancient "problem of the one and the many": they embrace everything and everyone in their vicinity. The embrace is the embodied withness of spirit. "Strong virtues come from almighty God, darting fire in divine glory; they ardently embrace [*ardenter amplectuntur*] and captivate those who truly fear God" (*Scivias* I.1.4; CCCM 43, p. 10). To embrace the sparks of virtue is to embrace nothing but their ardent embrace, to love (divine) love itself, as Augustine announces in his *Confessions*. Divine warmth set within Mary its embrace (*amplexionem caloris sui*), complicating the relation interiority–exteriority: the embrace into which Mary is called is within her. The grip of fiery spirit is that of matter on fire and as fire, of matter that accommodates all within itself. The gathering of matter and spirit is a gathering of two gatherings, a double cosmic embrace.

Our matter or mother, wood or the woods, on fire is matter hardly distinguishable from energy, a mother who is also, using classical Aristotelian terms, a father. The woods may certainly burn, as they do more and more frequently and devastatingly in the age of global warming, when a spark is enough to ignite them in extremely dry conditions. But, in themselves, they are already fire—the heat and the light of the sun captured, transformed, and perhaps decelerated. Fire can be quick or slow: we are not dealing with its presence or absence but with two heterogeneous pyro-temporalities. In a mélange of Heraclitus and quantum physics, we might say that the world of matter we take to be stable is mostly made of slow fire, while what we readily identify as raging fire is quick. Vegetation is slow fire in a winding series of negotiations with the quick solar blaze. Our world is a footnote to these negotiations.

Returning to Hildegard: the vegetal irradiations of Mary and Jesus are bolstered with the addition of fire to the tree image of the soul we have attended to earlier. In the same vision where the analogy between the powers of the soul and a tree makes its appearance, the soul is said to be "burning with a fire of profound knowledge" and to borrow its "two principal powers like arms, intellect and will," from those of fire: "For the soul gives life to a body as fire floods darkness with light [*velut ignis lumen tenebris infundit*]" (*Scivias* I.4.18; CCCM 43, p. 79). Intellect and will are the psychic correlates of the main effects of fire, light and warmth. At the same time, they are emblematized by plant organs—a green branch and the flower blossoming on it, Mary and Jesus. The verb *infundit* (floods) describes both the effects of fire and *viriditas*. The fire of the soul that floods into the body is liquid, that is to say, feminine and masculine, an indeterminate, volatile union reflected in its thermic and luminous "powers," along with their corresponding tactile and visual sensory registers.

Fire pervades our vegetal psycho-physiology. The profound knowledge Hildegard invokes is not purely theoretical: if the soul is burning with the fire of this knowledge, then it spreads luminosity and emits heat. The intellect is—nowhere near a passively contemplative feature of the soul—one of the active psychic forces, an arm together with the will, "baking each deed as though in a furnace [*voluntas es velut ignis quodque opus quasi in fornace coquens*]" (*Scivias* I.4.21; CCCM 43, p. 81). It does not culminate in the full illumination of that which is known, since the smoke of a raging fire also shrouds the source of the conflagration. Thus, a secret alliance of light with obscurity is preserved here as much as in the world of plants that span the darkness of the soil and the bright expanses of air.

The "arms" of the soul are its limbs that have imperceptibly mutated into a human shape, through the limbs (branches) of a tree, from "three little torches [*tres faculas*] arranged in such a way that by their fire they hold up the globe lest it fall" (*Scivias* I.3.4; CCCM 43, p. 43). Hildegard unequivocally ties the image of the torches to the Trinity, mingling its vegetal, fiery, and psychic versions. There are, nevertheless, only two powers of fire and two arms of the soul. So, how does a Trinitarian vision hold for igneous elemental reality? To put it briefly, Hildegard adds (without adding anything substantive) a third power to the conventional two; that third power is vigor, vivacity, liveliness: "In one fire, there are three powers [*in uno igne tres vires habet*]": it consists in "fiery heat [*igneo ardore*]," in "brilliant brightness [*splendida claritate*]," and in "implanted liveliness [*insitum vigorem*]" (*Scivias* II.2.6; CCCM 43, p. 128). The first power designates the Holy Spirit; the second, God the Father; the third, the Son, vegetal and igneous at once. Where there are two, the third always presents itself, as their interrelation, putting the dyad in motion.

We are still pursuing the thesis, as startling as it is almost self-evident, that plants not only are nourished by solar fire but *are* this fire, modified, refracted, rethought, reinvented. The portion of vegetal psycho-physiology that accumulates the heat of fire is the root—the "universal root of all," the Holy Spirit. This, too, is an aspect of Hildegard's revolutionary technique, upturning and immanently recoding natural processes. If, as she sings in her *Symphonia*, *viriditas* is "rooted in the sun," then its roots are soaked with solar heat, engrossed in the sun without leaving any distance that would enable a visual relation to its energy. The association of roots with darkness is troubled, and yet it remains undisturbed: troubled, because they are immersed in the sun, rather than the earth; undisturbed, because they house the thermal power of fire, which is neither bright nor dim, but of another order than that of visual representations. It is from the place of concealment in the open, of vegetal exposure even in the thick of underground existence, that fire spreads, propagated as though by bulbs or rhizomes, with the mycorrhiza of mediators developing around its edges.

The kinship of plants and fire goes both ways: plants are the solar blaze modified, and fire is a growing, metamorphosing, and decaying plant. The roots of the fire-plant extend to areas previously untouched by them; fire spreads from spirit to spirit, as if by contagion. The igneous spirit of *Symphonia* is such that "human minds catch fire from you [*Mentes hominum de te flagrant*]" (27.2). In *Scivias*, it is "the kindler and illuminator of the hearts of the faithful [*accensor et illuminator cordium fidelium hominum*]" (*Scivias* II.2.5; CCCM 43, p. 128). The root of the spiritual plant—of a plant that is spirit—nestles either in our minds or in our hearts, and it takes root precisely by catching fire, by setting its new supports ablaze. But, rather than dry wood to be ignited, the human psyche that the heart and the mind metonymize is fertile soil, in which the plant of fire grows and which grows with it, imbibing its heat. Psychic life is the element (indeed, an ecosystem) that welcomes the fire-plant's developing roots.

The vegetal modifications of solar fire are becoming more and more concrete right before our eyes. In their every cell, plants celebrate the marriage of heat and moisture, of a blaze tempered with and abiding in the humid earth. Assuming that these physical qualities signify spirit and body, respectively, plants are the embodiments of embodiment, the green incarnations of incarnation. Our psyches, for their part, occupy the position of a moist and cool body with respect to the Holy Spirit that extends its hot roots in them. The soul is a mobile hinge that turns up or down depending on whether it is received by the body or whether it accepts the sparks of the Holy Spirit, just as the body receives the soul. *Viriditas* is this tempered fire that burns all the better, the less dryness it encounters on its path. That the Holy Spirit is "fire without any flaw of aridity [*ignis sine macula ariditatis*]" (*Scivias* II.2.2; CCCM 43, p. 125) does not imply that it is a perfect, pure fire. On the contrary, "without any flaw of *ariditas*," its virtue is that it is fire and not fire, fire and life-giving moisture, or simply life.

As kinds of fire, the plant and the Holy Spirit are subject to the test, to which everything is put: "Spirit is to be tested by spirit, flesh by flesh, earth by air, fire by water [*ignis per aquam*]" (*Scivias*

I.2.29; CCCM 43, p. 33). Being tested by the same (spirit by spirit, flesh by flesh) coincides with being tested by the other (earth by air, fire by water). This coincidence of opposites is life. What is the sense of the verb "to test" (*probare*), though? Does it not suggest that the tested must engage in an interminable dialogue with the testing—with itself or with the other, with itself as other to itself? Fire is, for Hildegard as much as for the German Romantic writer known as Novalis, a lasting dialogue with what is on fire, with what, following myriad tempos and rhythms, it heats and lights up, and what changes it, too, for instance, by painting it in shades of green or drawing a singular figure within its universal medium. Fire probes and is probed by what it ignites: by itself as the other.

The transformations of fire that return, in one way or another, to Heraclitus are reversible: fire is one among the things to be tested, but it is also the tester, as in the case of "gold that must be tested in it [*Aurum in igne debet probari*]" (*Scivias* I.2.29; CCCM 43, p. 33). The testing of gold is, as Marx would have reminded us, a probing of "the universal equivalent," of a material mediator, which, by bordering on an abstraction, puts disparate things in relations of commensurability. Sparkling in gold is an inverse image of the Holy Spirit: whereas gold *a posteriori* facilitates an abstract equation of concrete entities, the Holy Spirit—the flaming root of all—is the *a priori* shared source of everything con-crete, things growing with each other and with it. Coming from above and from below, fire is the universal test of universality not exempt from the exigencies of being tested as to its capacity to give or renew life.

If fire, in Hildegard's view, is the universal tester, the human is a universal testee. "The human should be examined more than all other creatures, and he should be purified through all creatures [*homo super omnem creaturam examinandus est, et ideo per omnem creaturam expurgandus est*]," she writes (*Scivias* I.2.29; CCCM 43, p. 33). The testing of the human is akin to that of gold: both are universal equivalents due to their status of the universal exception. Tested "through all creatures," humanity is really tested through the Holy Spirit, responsible for the creaturely all-ness, the shared root of living beings aflame with life. Which is to say that, fundamentally, humanity is tested through fire, like gold.

Another, more modest and ecologically sound, reading of Hildegard's exigency is also possible. The test to which a human being is put in every creature is a test by fire, the fire of life lit by, and difficult to tell apart from, the Holy Spirit. Is one tempted to extinguish creaturely existence by handing it over to spiritless cold, to nihilism as environmental devastation? To burn it up in the conflagration of *ariditas*? Or, on the contrary, to nourish the heat of life's root with one's own mind and heart, the sublime soil wherein this root may grow and gain strength? To be purified through all creatures is to uphold their vital heat and, through it, the source whence this heat emanates. Conversely, to fall into the temptation of extinguishing the fire of life—the temptation associated with *ariditas*—is to rebel against the Holy Spirit and the universality of the life it inspires. That is how a human, and, more consequentially, humanity at large, fails the test by fire. That is how we all fail in the age said to be of "global warming."

The testing fire of *Scivias* is a reincarnation of the ancient *pur phronimon*, the discerning fire that sorted matter according to kinds, with the noetic function blown up to cosmic proportions. So, deriving from divine power, "the fire of justice burns up sins against every injustice [*iudicialis ignis comburens peccatum in omni iniustitia*]" (*Scivias* III.1.12; CCCM 43, p. 340). Fire itself discerns between good and evil—rewarding, comforting, and protecting the former; punishing and purifying the latter.

Lest we think that this probing discernment is imposed onto deeds from the outside, Hildegard identifies a purifying fire with the good and situates it at a distance from noxious flames. "And as fire burns and leaves no impurity unconsumed," she writes, "or as a craftsman purifies [*puriora*] jewelry by fire to remove its rust, so too does the good purify a person [*bonum facit hominem purum*], melting the rust of wickedness off him" (*Scivias* III.2.11; CCCM 43, p. 358). There is a fire of the good lodged within the discerning fire of divine justice, and, as we will see, this fire rages against another one, full of harmful fervors and flare-ups that threaten to consume the world. Whatever it passes its judgment on, fire is, in the first and last instances, self-discerning: its consciousness is already a self-consciousness, mindful of its own degrees and kinds. It is to these that we turn next.

Combined with water in the tissue of *viriditas*, fire is "sweet" or "pleasant": as the Holy Spirit, it "sweetly burns in the minds of the believers [*mentes credentium suaviter urit*]" (*Scivias* II.2.6; CCCM 43, p. 129). By no means does "sweet burning" latch onto the virtue of moderation, however. Hildegard could not be clearer that tepid devotion and lukewarm commitment are the signs of spiritual poverty, incompatible with the "sweet burning" of the divine root. The wavering, the instability of mind (*instabilitate mentis*), is "like a lukewarm wind, which gives neither moisture nor heat to the fruits [*tepidus ventus es qui nec umiditatem fructibus affert, nec eis calorem inducit*]" (*Scivias* II.5.28; CCCM 43, p. 199). Such a mind provides the fiery root with a poor soil: it serves neither as a conductor for the root's heat nor as a dependable substratum in which to grow spiritual radicles. In effect, the elemental milieu for spirit suddenly changes—in a manner that will be paralleled by our understanding of climate shorn of associations with a place and tied to atmospheric phenomena—from the earth to the moving air masses (wind) that do not stimulate plant growth. Indicative of spiritual decline, tepidness is not preferable to extreme ardency. In its acceptance of entropy, it is not at all synonymous with the "sweetness" of burning. Despite its scorching effects, aridity may be essentially tepid, as in the expression *ariditatem tepiditatis* (*Scivias* II.4.3; CCCM 43, p. 162).

When the degrees of fire are just right, fire is just and not harmful. In her "Declaration" prefacing *Scivias*, Hildegard relates her experience of revelations: "Heaven was opened, and a fiery light [*igneum lumen*] of exceeding brilliance came and suffused my whole brain [*totum cerebrum meum transfudit*] and inflamed my whole heart and my whole breast, not like a burning but like a warming flame [*velut flamma non tamen ardens sed calens ita inflammavit*] (*Scivias* I.Praef.; CCCM 43, p. 4). While excessive in its brilliance and in the way it permeates the whole of Hildegard's being (this inaugural moment of a fire that suffuses [*transfudit*] is commemorated in the fire that floods [*infundit*] darkness and the body), the flame of revelation warms without burning and lights up her interiority and the world. Keeping its intensity, this fire protects, nourishes, and transforms her interiority above all. That it does not burn (*non tamen ardens*) is not a hallmark of its neutrality, of a lukewarm or even cold liberal tolerance extended to the other, but of an altered relation to desire and the will, which are the psychic imprints of ardency, of a burning.

Spiritual inception airs the otherwise conservative nexus of a physical conception pertaining to women's fertility and that of the earth. Suffusion with fire turns into the diffusion of fertile moist heat in the two bodies, the female and the terrene: "A woman from time to time becomes aware of moisture in her, which diffuses itself through her in the fluid of fertility with heat [*cum calore in ea diffundit*] . . . For if she did not have the fluid of fertility with heat, she would remain fruitless like dry ground [*sicut arida terra*]" (*Scivias* II.3.22; CCCM 43, pp. 147–48). Moist heat belongs to the possibilities of *viriditas*, the greening green signaling regeneration, thanks to the auspicious combinations of and interactions among the environmental conditions. Dry heat, separating spirit from matter, pertains to the state of *ariditas*. In Mary's immaculate conception fiery suffusion is diffusion: the physical event is, in itself, spiritual. Whatever the case may be, the test of fire, by fire, is meant to ascertain generative and regenerative potentialities that only come to light when it is ready to combine with what it is not (here: water).

A mix of water and fire is the elemental matrix of *viriditas*, which includes baptismal rituals. Baptism is rebirth "from the water of sanctification and the spirit of illumination [*renascatur ex aqua sanctificationis et Spiritu illuminationis*]" (*Scivias* II.3.27; CCCM 43, p. 151). Carried out through its moist heat and light, regeneration is the moment of generating a human from the animal and vegetal beings we are. Does such a transformation require one to repress the prehistory of the human, to stop "being inundated, as with water, with the vegetative spirit [*velut aqua, cum spiritu vegetationis suae inundans*]" (*Scivias* II.3.27; CCCM 43, p. 151)?

Upon a closer look, changes turn out to be immanent to water, to fire, to spirit, to plants. The entire process moves under the sign of *viriditas*, aligned with the logic of vegetality and encrusted in a phytotheological frame. After being irrigated and heated in a certain way, the human germinates, plantlike, from the animal and the plant. Fire and water, plants and spirit are not repressed but sublimated. Fire is the most sublime medium of sublimation and the sublimated message, too. It is a form of transformation, amenable to losing itself, perennially—for instance, when it mixes with water as it does in *viriditas*.

In a flood of light and heat—in its double excess—as well as in its restriction to life-giving moist warmth, fire is no longer and not yet fire; it is an overpowering liquid force, a blazing and fluid precondition for flourishing. The one is not one, for a plurality of reasons. In the standoff of *viriditas* and *ariditas*, conversely, the struggle of the ever fresh greening green against the deadening potential of desert heat is internal to the one at war with itself. (Recall ancient *stasis* in this respect.) Just as the dirty waters of prehuman existence had to be washed off with the waters of baptism, so "noxious" fire must be countered with the fire of vegetal glory.

To fight fire with fire is the lot of those who, like us, confront within life a conflagration that rages against life, including the pyres of long-dead creatures burned in an unquenchable quest for energy. (A more sweeping hypothesis would be that living always entails an inner confrontation, as the objective—both organic and inorganic—supports of life betray it, at once expressing life and letting it down, expressing it in and as this failure that instigates finite existence to try again, and, according to Samuel Beckett, fail better.) The perverse resurrection, the reanimation in the flames of energy production and consumption of what had been fed with the sun and had long retreated into the earth, deadens the rest of the world. Past solar fire objectified in plant and animal remains that have ossified, liquefied, or gasified into fossil fuels briefly flashes again only to shroud the atmosphere and the earth with its fumes. It is relit in order, for an instant, to breathe life into industrial activity and then extinguish the conditions of possibility for life.

The appeal to fight fire with fire is at its starkest in the vision that opens book 3 of *Scivias*. There, Hildegard hears God saying to sinners: "In my zeal, I will kindle in you the fire of my wrath and burn up all your *viriditas* [*in zelo meo accendatur in te ignis indignationis meae, per quem comburam in te omnem viriditatem*], with which you tried to begin a work, trusting in your false energy [*in falso vigore*] . . . And I will burn up in you all your *ariditas*, that dryness which belongs to your sins [*comburamque in te omnem ariditatem illam peccati tui*] and that of the other lost ones, and in which you tempt humanity, which is ashes, to sin" (*Scivias* III.1.15; CCCM 43, p. 343).

In Mary, fiery suffusion was diffusion, physical conception being, *eo ipso*, spiritual; in the sinner, who, as a pile of dry wood, is prepared to be consumed by the flames of divine wrath, *viriditas* is *ariditas*, life is death, the forests of matter are experienced as nothing more than timber still before actual trees are felled. Sinning, as Hildegard construes it, is not a moral category, not disobedience in the face of God's commands, but a life lived against lives, against itself and against the future. Hence, the coincidence of opposites in it. The false energy (*falso vigore*) of a sinner's action is the future of no-future, *ariditas* masquerading as *viriditas* and, in the meanwhile, ensuring that freshness would vanish from the world, that nothing would germinate or regenerate ever again. Its dryness feigns a fire that, without a touch of moistness, is only fire, the fire reduced to its fake identity. This consolidated identity is what makes *ariditas* so fragile in its rigidity, so easy to enkindle with the devastating flames of divine wrath.

Although, physically, wet things are difficult to burn, spiritual strength is on their side. The moist warmth of cardiac and mental soil receives, as we have already seen, the Holy Spirit that "enkindles the hearts of his disciples with fiery tongues and makes them stronger [*incendentem corda discipulorum illius in igneis linguis, unde robustiores redditi sunt*]" (*Scivias* II.4.1; CCCM 43, p. 161). Hildegard indicates a subtle difference between the two events of catching fire by using distinct, if related, Latin verbs: *accendere* and *incendere*. A sinner is literally put to fire (*accendatur in te ignis*) and burns up starting from the outside; a disciple ignites from within (*incendentem corda discipulorum illius*), seeking to be oriented, motivated, and animated by the inner blaze. One is a fire that devours that wherein it burns, but without coming to an end and, instead, growing into an "eternal fire [*ignis aeternus*]" of damnation (*Scivias* III.1.15; CCCM 43, p. 343); the other is a fire that, in a finite existent, envisions a new beginning, another kindling, the regenerative movement of *viriditas*. Fighting fire with fire is also this: opposing the eternal with the infinite, the static reality of the same locked in its inflexible identity with the self-refreshing movement of finitude shedding its identity as a tree sheds leaves in the fall.

In the glory of virginity that protects virgin minds from harmful heat, we might detect yet another episode of fire fighting fire. Here, perhaps, it is the two powers of fire—light and heat—that are set against each other: the virgins "shining in the glory of virginity [*in gloria virginitatis fulgentes*] indicate that those who seek its [virginity's—MM] ranks should veil their minds from harmful heat all around [*mentes suas ab omni noxio calore circumtegant*]" (*Scivias* II.5.7; CCCM 43, p. 181). The shining glory of virginity creates a shield around the virgins in order to shelter them from the noxious ardor of carnal desire. It is a veil of light that protects the virgins (particularly, their minds!) against heat, in keeping with the view of the Holy Spirit as a protector, defender, or comforter, *paraclitus*: "O, fiery Spirit, the Protector [*O ignis Spiritus Paracliti*]" (*Symph.* 28.1a, 1).

If shining defends against heat, then the powers of fire split. An enlightenment prior to what would become known in Europe as the Age of Enlightenment, which would set the neutral light of reason against affective warmth, is wedged in this split. But the comforting shine of glory is poles apart from the dispassionate luminosity of pure reason, because, unlike the latter, it maintains a connection to the shadows, to concealment, to intimate obscurity. A *veil* of light does not aim to denude entities, baring their essence before the faculty of knowing. While such a veil may be seen, it does not let the gaze see through it. It resembles a tree canopy, the solar blaze filtered through the greening green of *viriditas*, which should not come as a surprise, since, *viriditate plena*, the Virgin is vegetally glorious and linked, by analogy, to the intellect. The shining light of virginal glory is interspersed with shadows: pitting fire against fire, it shields those swathed in it from desert heat.

Then, there is the oppositional fire *par excellence*: that of the devil, who "emits in the cruelest flames the terrible and manifold evil of his wicked counsels [*pessimum et multiplex malum crudelissimi incendii iniquae persuasionis emittens*]" (*Scivias* II.7.12; CCCM 43, p. 316). He injures humans, "burning them with the harmful heat of vices [*noxium ardorem vitiorum*]" (*Scivias* II.7.17; CCCM 43, p. 319). The excessive heat of "lust and voluptuousness" is to blame for this situation, but a good remedy is not cooling down or turning down the excess of heat (even if in *Physica* Hildegard will advise those with a "fiery" constitution not to consume hot foods that might further exacerbate the excesses of their thermal psycho-physiology). Psychoanalytically speaking, one might deal with the cruelest, crudest flames by refining and sublimating them, twisting or untwisting the source of an injury into a cure. Fighting fire with fire is, as the expression itself has it, collaborating with fire, working or playing with it in the midst of a confrontation. Here, *with* means *against*, or else *against* is elliptically signified by *with*. The collaboration, committed to being-with even in oppositional arrangements, is a vegetal mode of behavior. Immanent transformation (sublimation) is an act faithful to fire and to plants as its living instantiations.

A flickering thread of sublimated fire that has guided us thus far brings us to the sensitive heart of the matter: desire, love, ardent devotion, the burning of passions. Hildegard's supplication in *Scivias* sheds light on these emanations of heat: "O human, only today you were a fiery furnace [*igneam fornacem*], burning fiercely in your flesh with carnal desires [*in carne tua fortiter in concupiscentiis ardebas*]. Who gave you so much respite [*tantum refugium*] that you could escape the great fire [*magnum incendium*] of your lust?" (*Scivias* II.5.42; CCCM 43, p. 212). The "fiery furnace" is, at least on a formal level, symptomatic of spiritual intensity, since physical heat expresses animation, involvement, and engagement, tying the knot of withness. Apathy and withdrawal are not something Hildegard would cheer for. Following her logic, one will find refuge from the burning of carnal desires not in their cooling down but in another passion that opens a fire escape route *within* fire. That route is, of course, the passion of Christ: "the strength of the passion of the Son of God flows burningly forth [*ardenter inundante*] and rises to the height of celestial mysteries, as the perfume of aromatic herbs diffuses itself upward [*in sublime diffundit*]" (*Scivias* II.6.1; CCCM 43, p. 232).

The ardent passion of Christ is, predictably, a medley of the liquid element and fire in *viriditas*. Not by chance Hildegard analogizes the upward diffusion of this passion to the perfume of aromatic herbs heated by the sun: Jesus reprises the sensory (olfactory) effects of Mary, of the greenest branch, in whom "solar heat has distilled / a fragrance like that of a balsam [*calor solis in te sudavit / sicut odor balsami*]" (*Symph.* 19.2). The power of spirit induces the synesthesia of green fragrant warmth. The perfume, moreover, rises like and thanks to heat; it is diffused upward (*in sublime*), charting the path of spiritual elevation. What Jesus's vegetal figuration and Mary's vegetal image have given to olfaction is the aroma that presses on with the upward movement of growth already undergone by the plant's above-ground portions. The structure of a repetition within repetition becomes intelligible once we are reminded that plants are the sublimations of solar fire, striving, therefore, in their aerial parts toward that which they have sublimated. The cruelest flames of desire are sublimated in a human—or theandric—rehearsal of that vegetal sublimation, which stages the drama of desire with regard to the sun.

The vegetal and the human transformations of fire merge in Christ precisely at the moment of crucifixion. Could this be one of the "secret celestial mysteries [*secreto supernorum mysteriorum*]" revealed on the cross? Hildegard sees Jesus "hung on the tree of his passion [*in ligno passionis suae pendente*]" (*Scivias* II.6.1; CCCM 43, p. 232). The wooden support, which the cross provides in its vegetal afterlife, suddenly comes to life as a tree. (That said, *lignum* retains semantic ties to firewood, which feeds the burning of the passions. The ensuing semantic shuttling between the woods and wood transpires in the conceptual neighborhood of matter.) This uncanny tree is not, for all that, separate from the figure it props up: it is *ligno passionis suae*, the tree *of* his passion shaped as a plant. *In the cross*, sublimations of the solar blaze and of human desire intersect, geometrically represented by its vertical and horizontal planks. *On the cross*, hanging (*pendente*) is the experience of the in-between, of being suspended between modes of being, kinds of life, abodes, spheres, worlds. Between the human and the vegetal, which is a (if not *the*) figure of betweenness, Jesus becomes divine. *Viriditas* swaying on a tree is the greening green hanging on green, drawing on green, and drawing it into itself, as itself.

In the shadow of the tree of the cross, animal desire lurks. Its sublimation is accomplished through plants by bringing *viriditas* to the background *and* leaving it in the foreground of action, that is, by rendering it as firewood, the woods, and fire all at once. The action in question here is passion—the Passion of Christ—and, therefore, an undergoing, the heat of the will coupled with sensory and other sorts of receptivity. With regard to the mode of behavior they entail, with regard to the stage where the drama of life and death is incessantly replayed, the passions are vegetal. A properly human desire is animal desire vegetalized. The self-consciousness of one's vegetality is a path leading to divinity, to resurrection, resurgence (*resurgere*), arising or rising again as a plant.

In an ecological vein, sublimated fire is preserving, not destructive: it nourishes vital creaturely heat with its own burning. In her hymn *O eterne Deus* Hildegard includes the lines: "O eternal God, / may it please you now / so to burn in love [*ut in amore illo ardeas*] / that we may become the limbs [*membra*] / you made in the same love [*que fecisti in eodem amore*] / when you begot your Son / at the primal dawn / before all creation" (*Symph.* 7.1–8). *Viriditas* is God's burning in love that, retaining its generative and regenerative impetus, is imparted to finite creation. "Primal dawn [*prima aurora*]" is the glow of this fire that precedes the dawn of the first day, a light on the verge, before first daylight setting the rhythms—tempos—of time for creaturely existence. *Viriditas* lets us revisit, however improbable it may sound, this beginning before what was *In the beginning*, the beginning, which is without either a beginning or an end.

The burning of divine love lets beings and being itself be. The test by fire, to which humanity is put, ultimately verifies whether or not we could let this letting-be be. But how can we experience the heat and the light such combustion releases? By becoming the limbs (*membra*) made in God's love, forged in a fire that lends cohesiveness to bodies arranged together, the fire that fine-tunes their resonances with themselves and with other bodies, with the soul and with souls. There is definitely a difference between becoming the limbs of an animal organism and those of a tree, subservient to the whole in the first case and semi-autonomous from it in the second. Be this as it may, to become the members of an unnamed body, which overlaps with and overflows the spatiotemporal edges of creation, is to become sublimated and sublime, to imbibe the "powers" of a fire that lets beings be by allowing them to be with— the others and themselves.

Going back to the verge that is Adam's rib will enable us to monitor sublimation and desublimation with reference to fire and vegetality. The vegetal aspect of the creation of Eve from a side of Adam is that she "was formed from a rib by Adam's implanted heat and moistness [*de costa insito calore et humore [suco] Adae, Eva formata est*]" (*Scivias* I.2.11; CCCM 43, p. 19). Hot and moist, the rib is the site of *viriditas* and of divinity. The formulation *insito calore et humore* (or *suco*) will be later recaptured in a slightly modified phrase, *insitum vigorem*, to which we have already attended, discovering in it a vegetal characterization of Jesus. A woman sprouts from a man, but, Hildegard hurries to add, with a cross-reference to 1 Corinthians 11:12, he also sprouts from her: "Woman is created because of man, and man is made because of woman [*Mulier propter virum creata est, et vir propter mulierem factus est*]" (*Scivias* I.2.12; CCCM 43, p. 21). Starting with Eve, women give birth to men. But, despite his unique origin shorn of a mother (unless the earth counts as such), Adam is not exempt from the axiomatic making of a man by a woman: he becomes a man (*vir*) retrospectively, only following the creation of Eve and in relation to her, that is, only after *viriditas* parts, partly departs from him, and returns in the form of the other—a woman, for whom *he* is the other. With the two giving birth to one another, the origin is displaced. Their mutual grafting defies a clear-cut beginning and is, in this, consistent with their vegetal provenance.

Jesus's "burning love [*ardentis caritatis*]" is similarly reflected in Adam's initial approach to Eve. Before the Fall, "Adam burned so vehemently with his love of Eve [*Adam in caritate Evae tam fortiter ardebat*]," writes Hildegard (*Scivias* I.2.10; CCCM 43, p. 19). If *caritas* (divine love) irradiates from Adam and from Jesus, that is because their fiery element within tends toward the same element outside them: Eve, in the case of Adam's implanted heat; creation and the creator, in the case of the flaming spirit Jesus incarnates. The ancient metaphysics of fire is operative in this scenario, in which the element strives to reunite with itself, so that love is synonymous with justice in a series of adjustments gathering elemental realities together.

Nonetheless, everything is extremely volatile on the verge, where the blaze of *caritas* may be internally converted (and, hence, perverted) into the "deadly heat [*mortiferus calor*]" of lust (*libido*) (*Scivias* II.3.27; CCCM 43, p. 151). Life changes into death, a lush forest into a desert. Justice gives place to injustice. Elemental fire evades its own destiny, seeing that the verge is the time-space of prevarication, of transgression (*praevaricatio*), of stepping over and going beyond. For a dialectician, this sequence of events culminates in the birth of self-consciousness. Hildegard's thought goes a step further: transgression transgresses itself. Beyond the beyond, one lands in a state of isolation, which—counterintuitively, perhaps—defines lust. The heat of animality oblivious to vegetality is deadly because it aims to use *viriditas* in such an exaggerated way that the vigor of the greening green would be finally used up, slipping into *ariditas*. The blaze of what Hildegard understands as lust reduces the last bridges between the present and the future, the self and the other, the self and itself, to ash. These, too, are the transformations of fire that blossoms into plants and humanity, among other things. The flaming flowers of evil, a variation on the theme of dark fire . . .

ANARCHIES

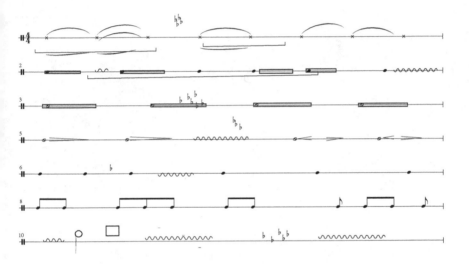

Anarchies only have the form that listening gives them. There
is no beginning and no end here. Different fragments are
set against each other and circulate freely in a space that has
neither limits nor directions. This movement/part may be
intercepted and crisscrossed with beginnings and ends at any
point, and it may last for an eternity. That the end arrives
and extinguishes the movement is just a coincidence.

9 mins 38 secs

Anarchies

I was going to begin this chapter with the following programmatic statement: "More often than qualifying God as eternal, Hildegard states that divinity has no beginning and no end. In this sense, God's infinity becomes anarchic, without a clear *arkhé*—without principle or principal, a unified point of departure that steers and controls the rest of a development. While bordering on negative theology, her persistent references to divine an-archy in *Symphonia* and elsewhere intersect with comparable assertions regarding plant life, the nature of *viriditas* that disrupts linear unfolding from a definite beginning to a determinate end."

I *was* going to begin this way, but I had to pull back to an earlier point, which is that the beginning itself has no beginning and no end. When it *is*, it is no longer a beginning but the middle of an ongoing process; when it *is not*, we find ourselves either, again, in the middle (ubiquitous, though excluded from the purview of formal logic) or at an end. Rife outside the beginning as much as within it, anarchy infiltrates into Latin in the guise of semantic lushness, with multiple nouns vying for the right to signify the beginning. Among these, *principium, initium,* and *caput* contribute the main colors to a palette of the concept's meanings, not least in Hildegard's writings.

Let's begin at the end of this brief but representative list, with *caput*, which unveils the beginning in the shape of a head. Treating martyrs as roses in the hymn *Vos flores rosarum*, Hildegard highlights in them the purpose (the end) that "endures before time [*manentis ante evum*]" (*Symph.* 38.8)—that is, before the beginning of the world. That purpose is, of course, the Son of God, who abides with the Father and the Holy Spirit in Trinitarian unity before creation, and who yields the absolute model for the martyrs' self-sacrifices. But what does "before time" convey outside a framework in which comparative terms *before* and *after* first make sense? Doesn't a slither of the temporal order distended beyond its confines introduce disorder and disorientation into distinctions between the created and the uncreated, the worldly and the eternal? Doesn't the endurance of the end before the beginning silently testify to this disorder?

More intriguingly still, the next two lines, invoking God, sing: *In illo, in quo non erat constitutio / a capite* (*Symph.* 38.9–10). These lines state *where* the purpose endures: "In him, who had no beginning." Read literally, however, the text is something of a motto of anarchic divinity. It says: "In him, in whom there was no order from the head." The words *a capite*—"from the head," as in the expression *a capite ad calcem*, "from head to heel"—are isolated from the rest on a separate line of verse: the head is cut from what is before and after it. Along these couple of lines, Hildegard distributes the two senses of the Greek *arkhé*: the principle as *constitutio* and the principal as *caput*, anticipating, preempting both with a *no* (*non erat*).

A headless, acephalic God is a point of approximation between Hildegard and Georges Bataille. It is, above all, God vegetalized, assuming that plants, too, lack a head, a vital organ that governs the rest of the organism as though it were the principle and the principal thing in their biological constitution. While a contemporary scientific hypothesis, reviving the work of Charles Darwin, postulates the equivalence of plant roots to the brains (the heads) of vertebrate animals, the dispersal of plant cognition along the entire vegetal organism, from meristems and leaves to root tips, corroborates the idea of being without a head. Plant-thinking, I have maintained ever since I coined this term, is also a thinking without a head, not reliant on the central nervous system and independent of any other sort of centralization. Vegetal ontology and epistemology are anarchic, which, in part, means that they are headless.

What does abiding in him, who had no beginning and therefore no head, entail? Hildegard is firmly convinced: it implies the act of rotating in a circle, the figure of divine infinity. God is "like a wheel [*quasi rotam*]" (*LDO* III.5.i; CCCM 92, p. 405), and "holy divinity" is "a circling wheel [*circueuntis rote*]" (*Symph.*, "O Fili dilectissimi," 3–4), its energy (*virtus*) "a circling circle, / encompassing all [*circuiens circuisti, / comprehendendo omnia*]" (*Symph.* 2.2–3). The circle is in the middle at every single point, none of them elevated over the rest. "Encompassing all," it does not seize beings from the outside, besieging them, as it were, but embraces and comprehends each wherever she, he, or it is. To abide in it is to be in the middle, in the midst of an anarchic, vegetal-messianic milieu. To exist.

In her visions, Hildegard sees the circle as a "brightly shining crown [*in modum coronae multo fulgentem*]" of "radiant divinity." God is "he who has a true circle [*vero circulum*] in a form of a brightly shining crown on the head [*in capite*]: that is the majesty of God, lacking beginning and end [*hoc est quod maiestas Dei initio et fine carens*]" (*Scivias* II.9.25; CCCM 43, p. 539). As it often happens in Hildegard's texts, dividing against itself, the beginning splits open: absent in the form of *initium*, it seems to be reinstated as *caput*, bearing a majestic crown, which is unmistakably echoed by *Keter* in the Jewish Kabbalah. Although the head reappears in order to serve as a support for the crown, although order in its cosmo-political splendor is momentarily restored, the beginning is undermined. Hildegard automatically assumes that the crown is to be worn on the head. She forgets that, in a beginning without beginning, the crown's circle retraces the shape of a missing head, giving no more than an indication, a promise, or a reminder of the head's existence. Vegetal-divine majesty is a crown for no-head, a splendid mark of anarchic power.

From the sphere of cosmo-politics to ethics, the head is superseded by the circle placed upon it. When, instead of divine *maiestas*, Hildegard sets her eyes on God's *benignitas*, she substitutes for the circle of the crown that of the halo: "That there is a circle above their heads [*eodem circulo supra idem caput*] . . . means that the faithful are saved by the most excellent goodness of Divinity, which is without beginning and end [*benignitas divinitatis, qui sine initio et fine est*]" (*LDO* I.1.iv; CCCM 92, p. 51).

The circle of the halo is another beginning, a principle and principal thing tied to, as much as it is separated from, the roundness of the head it envelops. The highest part of the body, the first corporeal element seen from above and the closest to the sky, is no longer what it was. A spherical symbol of the beginning (let it be noted, in passing, that its roundness immanently puts in question the beginning it symbolizes), the head is deposed by a sign for what is itself without beginning and end. The halo protects, as though with an ethereal sheath, at the same time as it dislodges that which it protects. It does not instigate a battle of principles and principals: spirit *versus* matter; a disembodied mind *versus* the body. Rather, because comparisons are absurd given the incommensurability of the terms—the heights—participating in them, the head is dethroned by the infinite, not by the highest.

❧

Condensed in the creative Word, divine prescience exhibits the shape of a circle. It, too, is "similar to a wheel [*in similitudine rote*]"—an "all-encircling whole [*cuncta circueuntis*]," "that admits no beginning nor is overthrown in the end [*que inicium non accepit / nec in fine prostrata est*]" (*Symph.*, "O Verbum Patris,"

11–14). Its circular infinity is not only spatial but also temporal: the foreknowledge of the future in the past generates a time loop. A recurrent, ringlike temporal structure is familiar to us from the course of calendar years that relay the rhythms of cosmic rotations (in the Justinian *Digest* a year [*annus*] is defined as "the duration of the motion, by which a planet revolves through its orbit [*mora motus quo suum planeta pervolvat circulum*]" [*Dig.* 40, 17, 4, 5]). Relatedly, the seasonal time of plants is a circle—revolving between seed and seed, or between spring and spring—ensconced within the circle of planetary time. The Word of God is verdant, but plant verdancy is divine, in that it is also "similar to a wheel." There is no beginning attributable to the first seed, nor is rotting the end at which a plant would be "overthrown [*prostrata*]," even if it lies prostrate on the earth with which it is about to fuse, since decay nourishes a future growth and gives a preview of another arising.

(I submit that the phases of plant existence alternating between vegetative growth and reproduction flesh out the two models of infinity, which Hegel dubs *bad* and *good*. The "bad infinity" of growth between germination and flowering is the infinity of a straight line tending outward without end in the sense of closure. The "good infinity" of reproduction is the circle of a plant returning to itself as other to itself, as a seed that issues from it. An unexpected conclusion, which follows from this vegetalization of infinity, is that the divine wheel is only one half of the phenomenon, oscillating between two figures of the infinite: a circle and a straight line.)

Throughout her works, Hildegard repeats, like a mantra, the idea that God is devoid of beginning and end. Nonetheless, she resorts to two main forms of expressing this idea: (1) proclaiming God to be "lacking beginning and end [*Deum initio et fine carentem*]" (*LDO* III.5.ii; CCCM 92, p. 407); and (2) defining God as "life without beginning and end [*sine inicio et fine vita est*]" (*TOQ* I, *solutio*; CCCM 226A, p. 111). The difference between *carens* and *sine* (or *absque*), between lacking something and being-without, is not trivial. Despite their shared attachment to negative theology, to a plenitude so unimaginable and ineffable in human terms that it lapses into its opposite when put into language, these words stress distinct aspects of divinity and of that which they negate.

On the one hand, the lack of finite, creaturely characteristics is the underside of another order of having, a possession of awesome powers—for instance, "enabling the existence of all and showing the good as the end of all [*mitem in operibus suis existentem, et ad omnia bona paratum ostendit*]," in the continuation of the passage I've cited in (1), or "having great brightness," as in "divinity that lacks the beginning has great brightness [*divinitas, que initio caret, magnam claritatem habet*]" (*LDO* III.5.i; CCCM 92, p. 406). On the other hand, being without beginning and end is not having anything else, but simply being alive, if not *being life*. Besides the fragment cited in (2), Hildegard ascribes the following affirmation to God in a letter to the monks of Mulenbrunnen (Maulbronn): "I am one who lives without beginning and without end [*Ego qui sine initio et sine fine vivo*]," evoking in the same lines the image of a "rotating wheel [*circueunte rota*]" (*Epist.* CLXXIIIr, 18–21; CCCM 91A, p. 393). It is through life, by way of the figure and promise of vitality, that the anarchy of divine without-beginning percolates to the rest of existence.

Life, then, is anarchic. It is lived, as we have discovered, in the middle, without beginning and end, regardless of the objective and irrefutable propositions that one is born and one dies. (These propositions actually become much more uncertain when applied to plants.) For the living, every point of a life is its midpoint; the living are invariably in life, which is also in them. In a sense that is not at all pejorative, the living are in a circle of life, in the midst of it from the very beginning without beginning. There is no *going into* this circle—*in-ire*: the verb form, from which *initium* derives—because one is always already in it. What is said about God is, by the same token, an appropriate elucidation of life: "God is in all creatures, exceeds all creatures, and neither beginning nor end can be found in him [*Deus in omnibus creaturis est omnesque creaturas excedit, quoniam nec inicium nec finis in eo reperitur*]" (*LDO* II.1.xxxviii; CCCM 92, p. 318).

Being without beginning and end is the excess within, animating the living at each moment of their life and precipitating their vitality. The greening green of *viriditas* is its synesthetic manifestation. When it came to creaturely existence, God "had his will in *viriditas* [*in viriditate voluntatis sue habebat*]" (*LDO* III.5.ii; CCCM 92, p. 407). But, in a circle, the past tense of *to have* blends with the future: touched by the infinite from within, as the indwelling of divine will, *viriditas* turns infinite, is infinitized, and, as a result, renders infinite whatever else it touches, from within or from without. *Viriditas* is the memory of the immemorial, a vestige of divine anarchy that discreetly refreshes the world, without the pomp of its "initial" creation.

With respect to the divine predication of life, the beginning, inscribed in *initium*, shatters, splitting against itself in the same word. "God alone is life [*Deus solus vita est*]," writes Hildegard, "and all that lives is moved by him, who alone is beginning without beginning [*quoniam ipse solus inicium sine inicio est*]" (*LDO* III.5.xxxii; CCCM 92, p. 455). *Inicium sine inicio* dilutes the purely negative form of *sine inicio*. If it leaves something of the beginning intact, then this intactness exacts a high price: the beginning is now shorn of its identity. The beginning is and is not God, right at the moment when God is defined through life, setting all that lives in motion. A straightforward explanation for this fissuring is that God, who is not and has no beginning, endows everything and everyone else with the beginning: "I am the one without beginning, and the one from whom all beginnings proceed [*Qui sine inicio sum et a quo omnia inicia procedunt*]" (*LDO* I.4.cv; CCCM 92, p. 248). He is, in a thinly veiled reference to Aristotle, the immobile ground for movement. Hildegard, however, sets her sights on a certain kind of movement here, namely growth.

The ground is divine soil, on which everything arises from below, springs up, burgeons like (and including) plants. It is "God, who lacks a beginning and by whom all creatures arise [*quod inicio caret, et quod per ipsum omnes creature surrexerunt*]" (*LDO* I.4.cv; CCCM 92, p. 259). Elsewhere, in a highly metaphysical mood, Hildegard is more emphatic still concerning the absence of growth and decay in divine realities: "God, who lacks beginning and end, suffers neither increase nor deterioration and is immutable [*Deus inicio et fine carens, nullum augmentum, nullum detrimentum recipit, quia inmutabilis est*]" (*ESSA* 419–20; CCCM 226, p. 124). The lack of beginnings and ends is presumably tied to the negation of growth and decay, even though these processes themselves are devoid of ends and beginnings. A deeper problem, though, is the transition from divine anarchy to the creative inception, from God *having* no beginning to *being* the immutable soil that warrants all growth, from the abyss of life to a precondition for living. How does Hildegard resolve this problem?

In a gesture that will be crucial to the fourteenth-century Byzantine theologian Gregory Palamas, Hildegard demarcates the differences between divine essence and divine existence, the energy of God rotating in itself and the energies that put the world into work or into play. In Hildegard's theological cartography, longitude is "divine essence, which is without end and beginning, and by the work of which all else has a beginning [*divina essentia, que sine fine et inicio est . . . quoniam ipsa ab opere suo, quod inicium habet*]." Latitude is "the infinite power of God [*infinita potestas Dei*]" (*TOQ* XV, *solutio*; CCCM 226A, p. 118). So, divine essence *is* without end and beginning, while its operationalization, an energetic putting-to-work, allows the world to *have* a beginning (*inicium habet*). In fact, the being of a work implies having a beginning (and an end) and, indeed, having this beginning outside the work itself, in the other. A created order emerges from divine anarchy when the energy circulating in divine essence discharges a series of works, firing into existence. A beginning becomes possible on the basis of no-beginning, and it persists, it holds tight in life, by virtue of this anarchic precession of their origin inculcated into the creatures.

For the work of creation to take off from the ground, concocting the soil for existence from the divine abyss, a mediation is required. That mediation is the creative Word, which was "in the beginning"; *In principio erat Verbum*, Hildegard quotes from the Gospel of John (1:1) in her *Liber divinorum operum* (*LDO* I.4.cv; CCCM 92, p. 248). The beginning divides against itself otherwise. The Word that was *in principio* is *sine initio*: "my Word has always been and is in me without beginning [*verbum meum, quod sine initio semper in me fuit et est*]" (*LDO* I.4.cv; CCCM 92, p. 248). It acts as a window or a doorframe, through which a negation of the beginning passes into its affirmation, and vice versa. Still, it is a window to exteriority *within* God (*in me*), a dawn of time suspended in timeless anarchy. To gather itself into a beginning, if temporarily, the Word needs to seize something for the first time from existence without beginning, to pre-take (*prae-capere*) something, to pre-understand, to set up a principle. That "something" is, perhaps, being itself in the third-person imperfect indicative of the verb *esse*, which is the *erat*, "was," of John 1:1 (compare this to the third-person perfect indicative of the same verb, *fuit*, describing the being of the Word in God in Hildegard's text). However authoritative, the seizure of the principle, the first seizure that *is* the principle, must at some point loosen its grip and let go, as the beginning crops up from and fades back into what is without beginning.

We have imperceptibly intruded into the territory of the beginning configured as *principium*, which asserts its sovereignty by taking hold of and taking over in advance all that ensues in and from it. Ostensibly the most powerful, this kind of beginning is tenuous, since the fist that grasps what is to commence—and, in grasping, calls it into being—will eventually unclench, its contents slipping away. The creative Word, channeled through the Holy Spirit, is in a privileged (negative) relation to *principium*, but so are, also, the remaining hypostases in the Trinity with respect to other instantiations of the beginning: God the Father is without *initium*, and the egalitarian Son is without *caput*. A Trinitarian version of divine anarchy gradually crystallizes before our eyes in a triple negation of the beginning, the outlines of which everywhere shadow creation.

The claim that the Word has a negative relation to *principium* may sound odd, particularly if voiced right after citing John 1:1, *In principio erat Verbum*. To better appreciate this relation, we should track the division of *principium*, its fecund splitting open (against itself) homologous to a germinating seed. Just as God the Father is, in his imbrication with life, *initium sine initio*, so the Word is *sine principium ante principio*, "without beginning before the beginning." Hildegard writes: "The Word was apart from the beginning of its [creation's] inception [*erat Verbum absque principio illius incoeptionis*] . . . The Word was without beginning before the beginning of creation, and in that beginning itself was the Word, and this Word before the beginning, and in the very beginning of creation, was with God [*Nam sine principio ante principium creaturarum et etiam in principio ipsarum erat verbum, et idem verbum ante principium et in ipso principio creaturarum erat apud Deum*]" (*LDO* I.4.cv; CCCM 92, p. 251).

The anarchy of the Word is such that it transgresses the boundaries, neither temporal nor extratemporal, between the beginning and what is without beginning, between a principled position and existence free of principles, between creation and the uncreated. Thanks to its anarchic constitution, the Word smuggles the *sine principio* into the *principium*, being before and after the world into the world's inception. If, as I have demonstrated earlier, the Word imparts the greening green of *viriditas* to creation that keeps resounding with it and, all the while, re-creating itself, that is because the lines separating the beginning from its absence have been erased *in the beginning itself*.

There is something mysterious in the winding paths of the Word, which is simultaneously without and before the beginning, apart from the beginning and in it. This mystery is not at loggerheads with rationality: harking back to the semantic creases of the Greek *logos* that have been smoothed out in the Latin *verbum*, Hildegard insists that "the Word is in rationality, because rationality has the Word in itself [*verbum in racionalitate est, quoniam racionalitas verbum in se habet*]" (*LDO* I.4.cv; CCCM 92, p. 250). Being and having coalesce in the relation of rationality and the Word, because this relation is relationality itself. It has relation for its content and form; thus, it *is* relation.

The anarchy of the divine Word is thoroughly rational, in that it is thoroughly relational. To gauge this, it is enough to observe how *with* and its underside, *without*, multiply in proximity to the Word. Indeed, the Word is a gateway between the beginning and no-beginning, inasmuch as it is with God and with creation: inasmuch as withness prevails in it above all else. Symphonic, it goes so far as to forge a relation between the essentially relational, tightly interwoven world and the essentially nonrelational absolute. The anarchic Word is the medium, through which the sound of the divine voice (another sense of the Greek *logos* we have already encountered in these pages) that is life passes into the voices of "his works, expressing, crying out, and singing [*opera sua sonando, clamando et cantando*]" what they are (*LDO* I.4.cv; CCCM 92, p. 251).

In all its vibrant, orotund, and sonorous actuality, the Word transposes the problematics of the beginning onto the vocal register. A sound without beginning and end resounds with and in the sounds of a limited duration, the voices that creatures have and that they ultimately are. While the voices resound each with itself, with the others, and with the anarchic sound of the Word, they are infinite. Being interlaced with the *with* impregnates them with infinity despite, and in the midst of, their finitude. The anarchy not only of the beginning, but also of the end.

Negated in infinity and affirmed in finitude, the end is not said in one manner only, in the same voice, with the same timbre and inflection, using the same word. In this, it mirrors the beginning, which is uttered in many different ways even in the same language. More precisely, each rendition of the end is indexed to a version of the beginning—a pairing that, within finitude, redraws the anarchic circle of God's infinity. So, "just as eternity before the beginning of the world lacks a beginning [*ante principium mundi initio caret*], so, also, this finite world has no end [*etiam finito mundo finem non habet*]. But the beginning and the end of the world make something like an all-embracing circle [*principium et terminus mundi quasi uno circulo comprehensionis concluduntur*]" (*LDO* III.5.ii; CCCM 92, p. 407).

Both *initium* and *principium* have their companion terms in the end: the former is paired with *finis*, along with which it is negated for being inapposite to divine nature; the latter joins *terminus* as an attribute of the world. Besides the anarchic circle of God reemerging in the world's closure, where *terminus* returns to *principium* (unless it is *principium* that surrenders its power and dissolves in *terminus*), the end (*finis*) that God lacks is equally missing in a finite world. The phrase "*finito mundo finem non habet*" is a wordplay that surreptitiously makes this finite world in-finite and, if the pairing of *finis* with *initium* is to be believed, deprives what has been initiated of its impetus, its inceptual impulse. What accounts for this double divestment of the finite world, denied its finitude by an immanent negation of the end and by the circle in which *principium* and *terminus* revolve?

Traversing the cracked and semi-arid terrain of the beginning— itself a cracking, a bursting open unto the anarchy of no-beginning, which is what is the lushest in it—we cannot help but take note of a power anomaly in *principium*. On the one hand, the first capture—or, maybe, capture preceding the series that could lend itself to a count beginning at *1*—is a principle and the principal thing. Its authority, however, is weak: the first seizing already seizes nothing, that is, nothing but the end. On the other hand, as a gateway, a threshold, or a verge between the creaturely realm and what has predated it, *principium* is the channel, through which divine power (*potestas*) passes into existence in the guise of *viriditas*. *Principium* must be stripped of its power so as to serve as a conduit for another power, if not for the very power of power, expressed in a self-regenerating actuality. Along with the creative Word, this version of the beginning wreaks havoc in and, at the same time, underwrites the dynamic architecture of the world. It clusters together the anarchic influences that maintain this world, which does not *have* but *is* an end, by letting it renew and replenish itself in in-finite finitude.

Anarchy: the beginning has rebegun and keeps rebeginning over and over. In this sense, *ariditas* is a promise of perfect order, of a well-delimited *arkhé*, when the beginning finally ceases and desists from its iterations, drifting back to the past.

Through the self-displacing principle of the beginning, divine power (*potestatis Dei*) leaves a mark on "creaturely plenitude" and on human hearts: "The future dispositions of God's perfect power were revealed, within creaturely plenitude [*cum plenitudine creaturarum*], as *viriditas* embedded in the germination to come of seeds [*viriditatem venturi et processuri germinis*] . . . as much as the *viriditas* with which the Holy Spirit inflamed human hearts [*Sancti Spiritus cordi hominis viriditatem inferunt*]" (*LDO* III.5.ii; CCCM 92, p. 409). The anarchy that is one and the same as God's perfect power turns the beginning into a matter of the future, of re-creating the principle of things over again by the things to come. Projecting its repetitions ahead has the effect of toppling and supplanting the absolute beginning, the inimitable starting point that remains forever in the past. In the ensuing anarchy, the beginning is always first and never first: it is and is not itself.

A deranged beginning, beside itself in itself, is *how* divine power is revealed in the finitude of existence. Hildegard also indicates *what* that power is revealed in: seeds about to sprout and the blazing human hearts that host the Holy Spirit. These are the vehicles of *viriditas*, the space-time capsules of the greening green, which grants them their fecundity. They are joined, too, by the elemental repositories of divine power that hand this power over to visibility: "Just as the soul, which, invisibly filled by the creator with his power [*potentiam*], visibly moves the body . . . so also the God of all creatures . . . invisibly brings out their possibilities out of the *viriditas* of the earth, and the heat of air, and the humidity of water [*possibilitatis sue vi ex viriditate terre et aeris calore, sed et aquarum humiditate*]" (*LDO* I.4.xli; CCCM 92, p. 177). *Potestas* mutates into *potentia* as it inches closer to and touches living beings, in whom it manifests itself as their possibility (*possibilitas*). If, among these possibilities, as environmental as they are spiritual, *viriditas* comes first, that is because it epitomizes the deranged beginning of life's anarchic reanimation between *potestas* and *potentia*, the *how* and the *what* of revelation, the recurrence of what has been and a verge of the unknown.

Where and when do we begin, according to this scheme of things? As in the case of plants, our possibilities are both inside and outside ourselves: in the resonance of the body and the soul, in their covibrations with the world and with the divine. The time of the possible is as twisted as its space. While existential possibilities are oriented toward the future, they hail from the immemorial past, preceding our conscious capacity for representation and time-consciousness itself. They mimic God's "dispositions that were futural [*dispositionibus que future erant*]," the past and the future closing the circle of time (*LDO* III.5.ii; CCCM 92, p. 409). From the perspective of God, the future *was*, and the temporal expressions of divine power, whether as *potestas* or as *potentia*, inflect possibilities with the past. The result is a confusion of the tenses, of time and extra-temporal being, of that which has a beginning and no-beginning . . .

Further destabilizing *principium* as the beginning of and in time is the precept that "all God's works dwelled in his presence before the beginning of time [*Omnia quidem que Deus operatus est, ante principium temporis in prescientia sua habuit*]" (*LDO* I.1.vii; CCCM 92, p. 52). That is another ecology—the ecology of infinity. Anarchic, in revolt against the *arkhé-principium* of creation, it is ecology in the strict sense of a dwelling with the Word that, before the beginning, was with God and was God. As soon as the ecology of the infinite starts careening toward immutability and gives the impression of trivializing material existence, however, Hildegard rectifies these tendencies with reference to plant life and its elemental milieu. The vision of divinity before the dawn of time is "akin to trees or other creatures in the vicinity of water, who are reflected in it [*quemadmodum arbores vel alia creatura aquis vicina in ipsis videntur*]: though they are not corporeally there in the water, all their forms are apparent in it" (*LDO* I.1.vii; CCCM 92, p. 52).

We have here before us the speculative moment par excellence: a reflection without the thing itself that is being reflected, providing an iconic image of dwelling in the presence of God before creation. Remarkably, Hildegard relies on what Plato despises and tries philosophically to elope from—that is, the simulacra of trees, their likenesses. She places their reflections at the beginning, before the beginning announced in divine *Fiat*, as more faithful to being with God than the material world itself. She thus likens these likenesses to the truest vision of existence in the ecology of infinity. What could be more anarchic than that?

Vegetal reflections appear for a very specific reason in Hildegard's account: the greening green of *viriditas* mirrors divine power (*potestas Dei*) on the waters of existence. The image closes the circle, where the reflected and the reflecting *infinitely reflect each other* without beginning and end. A tree growing by the water is a little bit of a Narcissus, seeing not only everything in its vicinity but also its own image apparent on the aqueous surface. The vision *of* the tree means that the visible tree dovetails with the seeing tree, whose exquisitely sensitive photoreceptors put together a mosaic of colors and catch a broad range of wavelengths on the solar spectrum. Tree vision is anarchic: it begins neither from the object nor from the subject of the gaze but with both at once, emanating from and circling back to the visible/seeing tree.

❧

. . . I was going to begin . . .

KISSES

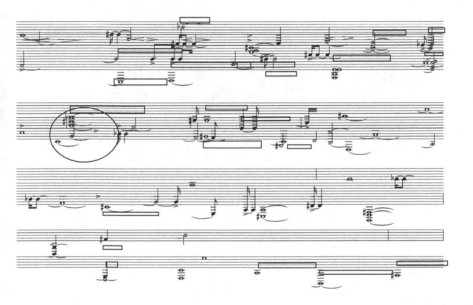

Touch, as when a hand touches a string through the bow, is a gesture that gives a feeling of close contact. The possibilities of a game on the two sides of contact are inexhaustible and can lead to a relationship between them as well as to a situation where no further contact is expected. It is made of brief touches that are never innocent but declare the desire for understanding. The string quartet that appears here was for a long time regarded as the ultimate form of ensemble playing. There will be an intimate low-key play between four parts that move out of the same material.

4 mins 22 secs

Kisses

THE FOLLOWING REFLECTIONS are occasioned by Hildegard's recurrent farewell message in *Scivias*. At the close of the last vision in book 2, she writes, as she will in concluding some of her other visions, too: "But let the one who sees with watchful eyes and hears with attentive ears welcome with an embracing kiss my mystical words, emanating from me, the living one [*Sed qui vigilatibus oculis videt et sonantibus auribus audit, hic mysticis verbis meis osculum amplexionis praebeat quae de me vivente emanant*]" (*Scivias* II.7.25; CCCM 43, p. 325). The reader or the listener is the subject of the kiss, the one giving a welcoming kiss to mystical words. The image is suggestive in the extreme. And here are some of the questions the kiss raises.

1. How is it possible to receive words with a kiss? When lips are articulated in an act of speaking, they do not plant a kiss on any surface—unless it is air itself that they kiss. Or, do "mystical words [*mysticis verbis*]" blend with the kissing lips? Do speech, silence, and the rugged edges between them change when the spoken word is mystical? How do the depths of mysticism come into contact with the surface they kiss?

2. The sites of reception Hildegard mentions do not include the mouth. Watchful eyes and attentive ears—that is, the exemplary

sense organs—welcome words with a kiss. Under a mystical lens, does the field of perception as a whole operate on the model of kissing? Is perception not triggered by external pressure, converted into sensory impressions? Is it activated, instead, by the lightest touch, skin to skin, by words and appearances, by the skin of words and the rind of appearances that together weave the world?

3. Whose mystical words are these? Hildegard's or those of God? Of both? What does it mean for the words that kiss and that call for the reciprocity of being kissed to "emanate from me, the living one [*de me vivente emanant*]"? Are these *speaking* words not *spoken*, not necessarily verbalized, because they are the expressions of the living? Are they the words of flesh—if not flesh *as* words—articulated in the fleshy language of mysticism? Is that why they don a mask of silence?

I will not pretend that I have the answers to all, or even to most, of these questions. They, along with a number of others they imply, will persist for the rest of this chapter, planting, perhaps, their kisses on the body of the text and of thought, on *your* eyes and ears. Hildegard herself makes the appeal to welcome her words with a kiss several times in *Scivias*—for instance, also at the end of the second and fourth visions in book 2 (*Scivias* II.2 and II.4). Kissing and being kissed once is not enough; nor is it sufficient to raise a question and attempt an answer on a single occasion. They demand the never-enough of a repetition, in the course of which the kissed or the questioned is experienced as that which, or the one who, cannot be revealed once and for all.

Although, as I have already indicated, I will not pretend that I am in a position to answer, comprehensively, the three blocks of questions above, I will channel their energy toward an outline of what I am tempted to call "an ecological theology of kissing." As Hildegard pictures them, creation and the knowledge of creation are interlaced through kissing: the kiss of God exuding the greenest green of *viriditas* and the kiss of the human mind through which the world becomes knowable. In the ecology of kissing, what doesn't seem to speak, and so is excluded from the traditional scope of *logos*, speaks the language of kisses. The kissing and the kissed dwell in the speaking of the kiss itself, in its fleshy/mystical grammar. That is their *oikos*. In philosophical terms, ontology and epistemology, being and knowing, are incorporated into the ecology of kissing; they are the manifestations of this ecology.

⤳

Hildegard's response to a letter from the prelates of Cologne contains some of the most invaluable bits that make up an ecological theology of kissing. "These," she notes, "are the materials for the instruction of humankind, who understand by touching, kissing, and embracing, since these acts serve them [*Hec sunt etiam instrumenta edificationis hominis, que tangendo, osculando et amplectendo comprehendit*]: by touching, because a man remains in them; by kissing, because he gains knowledge through them; by embracing, because he exercises his noble power through them. Without them, humankind would have no freedom of possibilities [*nullam licentiam possibilitatis haberet*]. So, they are with humankind, and it is with them" (*Epist.* XVr, 29–35; CCCM 91, p. 35).

The instruction, education, or edification of humanity is the construction of an ecological theology. The materials used for this edifice—touching, kissing, and embracing—are the acts of approximation and proximity, the kind of intimacy where, as in a certain interpretation of *philosophy*, loving and knowing are one. It would be wrong, for all that, to visualize the edifice as an independent structure, external to the humanity it houses. In emphasizing that the materials are "with humankind and it is with them [*ista cum homine, et homo cum illis*]," Hildegard is alluding to how the Word is with God before and during creation. Touching, kissing, and embracing are humanity itself and the only dwelling worthy of human being.

In Hildegard's sensuous wisdom of love, kissing corresponds to knowing. Without giving it a second thought, we usually—and on the contrary—associate a kiss with a lacuna in knowledge, a dark or semi-obscure space and time of getting so close to the kissed that we fail to see them anymore. Of shutting our eyes, maybe. Of having the lips and the mouth unavailable for the production of speech. So, what sort of knowledge does Hildegard have in mind?

The original sin forms a negative background for the model of knowing that, beginning in the mouth, travels down the winding paths of the digestive tract. Recall that it was starting with "the taste of the fruit he knew by disobedience" that Adam received the "harmful sweetness" of vice in his blood and flesh (*Scivias* I.4.5; CCCM 43, p. 68). Adam and Eve fatally erred when "they tried to know the wisdom of the law with their intelligence, as if with the nose, but did not perfectly digest it by putting it in their mouths" (*Scivias* II.1.8; CCCM 43, p. 117). The forbidden fruit was bitten into, chewed upon, tasted (barely), swallowed, destroyed—but not digested. Instead, the first humans were digested into death through it. But what if the problem were not so much the fruit itself as the way of knowing Adam and Eve pursued by its means, the knowing that rips into and devastates the other in an effort to assimilate its very otherness? Should this thesis hold, the plant, on which the fruit grew, would have to be renamed the Tree of Knowledge of Good and Evil *Knowing*.

The knowing a kiss affords could not be any different from digestive assimilation. A kiss is utterly superficial, gliding or brushing on the surface of skin, touched by the lips that are, themselves, covered with exceptionally sensitive skin. Kissed, the words and the world are not swallowed up by the knower, but loved and preserved in their independence. The knowledge that does not pass your lips has nothing to assimilate, either: the mystical kiss is welcomed in all its foreignness. The lips, sensitive as they are, draw a protective barrier over the threat our sharp teeth pose. Without putting anything in words, they say that the kiss is a "kiss of peace [*osculum pacis*]" (*Symph.* 25.8).

Save for some carnivorous outliers, plants eat nonviolently.

They kiss and are kissed by the sun and by water; without teeth or equivalent structures, they do not destroy living shapes to nourish themselves. By and large, they breathe and live on the surface, multiplying their leaves that are as much the plants' mouths as are the roots. And, just as a mouth need not have a shape recognizable as human or quasi-human, so the lips (that kiss and are kissed) need not be anthropomorphically familiar. In fact, their defamiliarization begins right on the human face.

Following Hildegard, eyes and ears, too, kiss the mystical words that arrive at their thresholds, verging on perception. The eyelids are, undoubtedly, kinds of lips, kissing and kissed by light (which they also filter out). With the ears, things are more complicated. They are not divided into parts that would allow them to close and open all by themselves: to stop hearing, one needs to shut them with one's hands or other objects. The contention that ears also kiss prompts us to think of lips otherwise. In the vein of this rethinking, lips are the delicate edges that kiss when they gently brush against other edges: leaves against sunlight and flows of air; flowers against butterfly wings and honeybee tongues and legs, and so forth. Plant-knowing is the wisdom of love, because, almost always, it knows the world by kissing. In its interactions with the elements, it opens a small window onto that world where everything kisses everything else and is in touch with everything else through the kiss.

The structure Hildegard sketches in a letter to the prelates of Cologne is a replica of her appeal to the readers of *Scivias* to receive her words with an "embracing kiss." The strange-sounding formulation *osculum amplexionis*, which I have translated as "the embracing kiss," puts together kissing and embracing, two of the three sides in the edification (dwelling and instruction) of humankind. The third term, to do with touching, is *praebeat*—a grammatical form of the verb *praebēre*, "to expose," "to present," "to

display," all of which are the preconditions for touching. Between
the receptivity of exposure and the active, though nonviolent,
involvement of the embrace, the kiss is a mediator, in the same
fashion that plants and Jesus are mediators, kisses in their own
right: of the sky and the earth, the human and the divine. Thus,
Hildegard's recurrent message at the end of some of her visions
exposes itself to, kisses, and embraces the edifice of humankind,
itself consisting of an exposing touch, kissing, and embracing.

The letter in question proceeds to analogize aspects of creation
to divine sense organs. "From him the wind blows, saying: lacking
no power, I have set the firmament with all its ornaments, with
eyes to see, ears to hear, a nose to smell, a mouth to taste. For the
sun is like the light of his [God's—MM] eyes, the wind like the
hearing of his ears, the air like his fragrance, the dew like his taste
exuding the greening green [*ros gustus eius viriditatem sudando*]"
(*Epist.* XVr, 9–15; CCCM 91, p. 34). What we know as a medium
for the senses (light for vision, air and its vibrations for smelling
and hearing, moisture for tasting) becomes the message, that is,
divine sensory activity. As they kiss Hildegard's (or God's) mystical
words, watchful eyes and attentive ears gain the ability to see and
to hear another dimension of sense, the sensory reality of what was
assumed to be no more than material possibilities for the human
senses. The entire world of the elements comes alive, a sleeping
beauty awakened by a kiss. Except that it was not the world that
was slumbering, but the eyes and the ears that were blind to the
seeing of light and deaf to the hearing of wind, among other facets
of the divine sensorium.

Of special interest to us is the environmental mouth of God
with its sense of taste embodied in the dew and exuding *viriditas*.
Yet, tasting is an early stage of assimilation and incorporation, a
harbinger of the knowledge that eats into things and eats them up.
The other, nonviolent, vegetal mode of knowing is prior to tasting,
the lips momentarily joining the inassimilable surface they kiss.
(That the kissed surface remains inassimilable ensures the mystical

nature of the words and knowledge involved.) The greening green, emanating from the divine mouth, is a kiss given to creation so that it would be capable of refreshing and renewing itself, regenerating. Far from assimilating the world to God's digestive tract, this kiss *imparts* a divine power to this world. That said, the gentle and generous impetus is not infinite: its capacity for renewal itself needs to be renewed. In the mystical repetition of the creation narrative, Jesus incarnates a kiss of divine and human natures, promising rebirth when the power of *viriditas* has catastrophically waned.

Behind the scenes of Hildegard's interpretation, as it bears on the theandric, lurks the twelfth-century representation of Christ as a kiss. In *Sermons on The Song of Songs*, pivoting around the verse "Let him kiss me with a kiss of his mouth" (1:2), Bernard of Clairvaux says: "The mouth that kisses signifies the Word who assumes human nature; the nature assumed receives the kiss; the kiss, however, that takes its being both from the giver and the receiver, is a person that is formed by both, 'the one mediator between God and mankind, himself a man, Christ Jesus'" (II.3). Hildegard, in turn, gives a voice to divine love (*caritas*) in a letter to Duno, Prior of Bamberg: "I sat inviolate in heavens and I kissed the earth [*In celo integra sedi et terram osculata sum*]" (*Epist.* LVIII, 24–25; CCCM 91, p. 138). Jesus is a personification of the kiss, which *caritas* gives to the earth, while remaining whole in heavens. Further, as Hildegard intimates in another letter, God the Father receives his prodigal children "with the kiss of the humanity of his son [*quem ipse osculo humanitatis Filii sui suscepit*]" (*Epist.* LXIIr, 8–9; CCCM 91, p. 145). "The kiss of humanity [*osculo humanitatis*]" is a kiss of humanity and divinity (*Filii sui*), a meeting or a crossing in the middle, between the soft edges of the kissing and the kissed.

Kissing is replete with the inflections, adumbrations, alterations of the in-between—of lips, edges, surfaces, skins, natures. It is an act always destined to the other, transpiring between the one and the other, for one does not kiss oneself. A province of plants and

of Jesus, the in-between defines the role and the being of mediators, spanning the soil and the sky, heavens and earth. The edges
of these domains are the lips turned toward one another, kissing
and kissed. The kiss itself, nonetheless, is what grows or otherwise
unfolds between them, as Bernard stresses in his sermon and as Hildegard makes clear in the figure of "the kiss of humanity." Distances
traversed, boundaries crossed, edges touching, and still difference
not abolished: "I sat inviolate in heavens and I kissed the earth."

As we have come to expect by now, the crossings Hildegard
signals in her writings are the sites of inversion, of sudden about-
faces, twists and turns. So it is also in the case of the divine kiss. The
obedient children of the church, Hildegard proposes to the Abbot
of Cologne, "are the kiss of Christ's mouth [*unde etiam obedientes
filii osculum oris Christi sunt*]" (*Epist.* CLVr, 22–23; CCCM 91A,
p. 346). We may surmise that the cumbersome expression *osculum
oris Christi* is not fortuitous: Bernard spends several passages in
his sermons on the Song of Songs developing an exegesis of the
words "with a kiss of his mouth," where he shows how the kiss is
separate from the lips that plant it and how it hovers, as it were,
between the kissing and the kissed. But, seeing that Jesus himself
is a hypostasis of the kiss, in which divine and human natures are
entwined, to be "kissed by the mouth of Christ" is to be kissed by
the kiss as such. There is no mouth behind this kiss, this mediation
of mediation, the middle of the middle where life belongs, finite
without beginning and end. Obedience is here not the obedience
owed to a figure of authority, sovereign and absolute, but that owed
to a singular universal mediation: to the kiss, to being-in-between.

Continuing her epistolary reflections, Hildegard writes: "Great
are the obedient disciples who are embraced by divine love [*in
amplexione caritatis*] and are not moved to wrath, those who are
the kiss of God and are fed bread made of pure flour [*quia osculum
Dei sunt et pane pure farina pascendi sunt*]" (*Epist.* CLVr, 23–25;
CCCM 91A, p. 346). Again, the three kinds of materials for the
edifice and edification of humanity are present in these lines: the

embrace of divine love, being kissed by God, and the patience of touch not easily irritated or angered. At the same time, the ecological instruction and comprehension hinging on a kiss flips into the incorporation of knowledge as nourishment, "bread made of pure flour." Why?

I see at least two reasons for the return to digestion.

First, in an allusion to communion and to Augustine's reading of this ritual, Hildegard hints that the interiorization of bread by those who receive a kiss from the mouth of Christ is, actually, an exteriorization, in a reflux to the community of believers. Fed the body of Christ, the believers are incorporated into that body. The act turning the digestive process inside out is the kiss.

Second, Bernard frames his interpretation of the Song of Songs in terms of solid food for spirit, which is none other than bread. "Be ready then," he says at the outset, "to feed on bread rather than milk. Solomon has bread to give that is splendid and delicious, the bread of that book called The Song of Songs. Let us bring it forth then, if you please, and break it" (I.1). But the textual/ spiritual bread Bernard breaks with his listeners and readers is the meaning of a kiss, notably of Christ as the kiss of humanity and divinity hypostatized. In strict adherence to the functional plurality of the mouth—which is for kissing, eating, speaking, occasionally breathing, and so on—the edification of humanity is a place for competing models of a knowing kiss to come into contact along their edges.

In the ecological theology of kissing, the world and what lies beyond its horizons come together in the lightest, as well as the most sensitive and sensuous, touch. (The horizon is the place or the non-place where the sky and the earth kiss.) While playing on the surface of things, with the surfaces and soft edges that eventuate the kiss in the times and spaces between them, Hildegard is engaged in the serious work of building a dwelling (*oikos*) for everything that is. That dwelling is nothing substantive. Relational through and through, it is situated, precisely, in a region of intermediacy, as a kiss distinct both from the kissing and the kissed.

Kissing involves, therefore, external surfaces and the momentarily bridged gaps between them. But what about interiority, the indwelling of faith and, in the Augustinian tradition, of God himself? Indeed, Hildegard sees in devotion to the divine "the kiss of the heart [*osculum cordis*]": "And so the person promises the thing to God with good devotion and just reverence, and offers himself to Him by a kiss of the heart, that is, by the will of his desire [*Et ita cum bona devotione et cum justa reverentia homo ille promittit Deo, illud ei offerens per osculum cordis, quod est per voluntatem desideriorum suorum*]" (*Scivias* II.5.48; CCCM 43, p. 216). A devoted soul receives a kiss from God right in its heart, at its very psychic core. According to a more radical interpretation, though, psychic interiority is born from that kiss, from "the will of desire" that turns inward and finds divine exteriority within the circle that this will closes. The intermediacy of the kiss percolates into and animates the depths of the soul, aired in its interstices.

The soul receives a "kiss of the heart" when it is out of breath, when it loses its innate connection to air, is consolidated in its self-identity, and no longer aspires to the other: "the breathless soul [*anhelans anima*], in its full knowledge, touches his [the devotee's—MM] good sense with the conviction that he should do a certain thing" (*Scivias* II.5.48; CCCM 43, p. 216). The kiss and the touch recall two of the dimensions of the human edifice and edification, whereas the third—the embrace of the other within—is their outcome. The kiss of the heart troubles the distinction between the inner and the outer, shedding light on the surface of depth itself, the exteriority of interiority that breathes through the pores. It alludes to the Pauline expression "the circumcision of the heart": "A person is a Jew, who is one inwardly, and circumcision is of the heart [*peritomé kardias*]—by spirit, not by the letter" (Romans 2:29). Without a trace of violence, which accompanies the act of physical circumcision, a kiss of the heart confirms that even our depth, whether bodily or psychic, is all skin. Exposed despite the hiddenness of intentions, desires, and stirrings of the will, it is to be caressed and brushed with lips, not cut and mutilated. The kiss of the heart, therefore, vegetalizes our profoundly animal heritage, sneaking exposure and superficiality into our psychic constitution.

The words "kiss of the heart" are uttered again in *Order of the Virtues* by the happy soul, *felix anima*. Addressing the virtues, she exclaims: "Oh, let me come to you freely so that you would give me a kiss of the heart [*O libenter veniam ad vos, / ut prebeatis michi osculum cordis*]" (*Ordo* 1, 32; CCCM 226, p. 506). The virtues then respond: "We must fight you, royal daughter [*Nos debemus militare te cum, o filia regis*]" (*Ordo* 1, 35; CCCM 226, p. 506). The contrast between a peaceful kiss and military activity could not be starker. The soul attributes the impossibility of receiving a virtuous kiss in its interiority to its being encumbered by the body, by the "heavy weight [*durum pondus*]" of corporeality, which is its "dress in this life [*veste huius vite*]" (*Ordo* 1, 37; CCCM 226, p. 506). And yet, without its bodily garment, the soul has no effectivity in this world, in this life, where it resonates with other bodies/voices. The freedom of a kissed heart resides not in its liberation from material reality but in aspiring toward its other, opening the surface of its depths to exteriority, be it that of God or of the body. For, just as vitality is made of the resonances of the body and the soul, so, in another sense—grasped with other senses, such as touch—it flourishes with the soul kissing the body, which kisses the soul back.

Hildegard, in effect, never tires of stressing the value of *this* life and *this* world. In one of her letters, she recommends "that in all your ways you praise God . . . cogitate on his precepts repeating them tirelessly, kiss him through faith [*per fidem osculare*], and embrace him through your good works [*in bonis operibus amplectere*] . . . And you will do these things all the days of your life, while you live in this world, so that afterwards you may live in an infinite world forever and ever [*et hoc omnibus diebus vite tue facies, quousque in hoc seculo vivis, quatenus postea in infinito seculo in eternum vivas*] (*Epist.* XLIIIr, 28–39; CCCM 91, p. 111).

The edification and the edifice of humanity—relying on touching, kissing, and embracing—are built in this world, in this life. They are ecological construction sites that cannot be neglected and left derelict, dwarfed by otherworldliness and eternity. Through the kiss of faith, which is an interiority thrust open to the exterior, and the embrace of good works, representing exteriority tending toward the interior, "this world you live in [*in hoc saeculo vivis*]" and the "infinite world [*infinito saeculo*]" touch, kiss, and embrace one another. Those touches, kisses, and embraces are the points of contact between theology and ecology—green mass in the flesh and of the flesh no longer at war with spirit, no longer at war with itself.

POSTLUDE

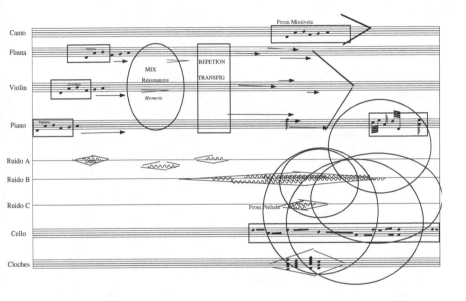

The Postlude is both the opposite of and the follow-up to the Prelude. Instead of calling forth and notifying listeners about what is coming, it puts the memory of the bygone at the center. The movement begins like a fugue, which will be taken over by a new world. Memory becomes a dream, and clangor asks questions that can only be left unanswered. The Postlude is a farewell where no final word can be said. The decrease that takes place is successive and ends at zero.

7 mins 42 secs

Postlude

As I am sure you have noticed, the book you have just read deviates from the usual structure of academic works. That is not to deny that I have relied, at times quite heavily, on such scholarly techniques as the exegesis, or close reading, of Hildegard's texts or on the contextualization of her ideas in the theological and philosophical traditions they communicate with. Regardless of these auxiliary strategies, the experimental method I have done my best to follow in these pages is thinking with Hildegard, without the demand to reconstruct anything like her authentic and authoritative thought.

More than any determinate subject matter, it is such an experimental method that I share with Peter Schuback and his musical attempt to resonate with Hildegard, through the themes I have focused on in *Green Mass*. As he writes in his Afterword, his composition does not seek "an 'authentic' or 'stylistically correct' practice of hers," something that would be impossible given the time that has elapsed since (and given, obviously, a lack of sound recording technologies in the twelfth century). Just as I have been thinking with Hildegard, Schuback has been listening with her, listening to a mode of listening her musical works opened up.

What does thinking with another look like? And, especially, with the other no longer alive, both accessible and unreachable through the numerous texts she has left behind?

There is no univocal answer to these questions, because thinking with the other is a singular event impossible to replicate in a dispassionate manner, to which the modern scientific method aspires. It matters not only who thinks on the two sides of the unique relation and how, but also around what such cothinking revolves. My thinking with Hildegard had to do with the workings of plant-thinking in theology, and, therefore, it revolved *around thinking*, around someone, rather than something to be merely thought. Thinking with her was, simultaneously, thinking with plants both at the level of substance and at the level of process.

The vegetal substance of Hildegard's thinking is concentrated in *viriditas*. The greening green allows the world to persist by regenerating itself in its finitude. Borrowing from and fully embodied in plants, *viriditas* creates a world that is *of* plants and that is, also, for nonplants. Besides renewing the conditions that ensure the vitality of animals and humans—conditions such as nourishment, fertile soil, or breathable air—the regenerative "green" power operates within them, instilling the promise of infinity in finite existence. Ongoing world-creation through *viriditas* is the exercise of thinking (here: plant-thinking, which has to be distinguished from rationality; and even rationality does not mean the same thing for Hildegard as it does in modernity, as we have seen), of *logos* that immanently steers the world through the moments of its growth, decay, and metamorphosis. Hildegardian eco*logy* is, thus, a way of interpreting and engaging with plant-thinking.

I have, nonetheless, set out to sketch Hildegard's ecological theology. How does the combination of theology and ecology work, given the centrality of plant-thinking in my thinking with Hildegard?

First, the regenerative *logos* of *viriditas* recalls and reignites the *Logos* of divine world-creation, not translating but transmitting its living memory. In the course of being transmitted, the creative

Word mutates, shedding many of its metaphysical features. The *-logy* part of theology and ecology is at once the same and different, the *logos* of the latter receiving and modifying the *Logos* of the former. *Viriditas*, as the site of eco-theo-logical plant-thinking, is an important catalyst in this receptive modification.

Second, as I confessed in the introduction to this book, "I feel particular affinity to Hildegard, in that I see her vegetalizing theology in much the same way as I've attempted to vegetalize the Western philosophical canon." Mary and Jesus hypostatize *viriditas* at the same time that they are the hypostases of divinity. "Ecological" is not one among many features of Hildegard's theology; it is, by dint of the vegetalization I have pointed out, the vital core of her theological project.

A vital core, in turn, is not to be conflated with the stiff and stationary foundations that Western thought clamors for. If the process of Hildegard's theology is vegetal, that is because the core itself grows, decays, metamorphoses, allowing us, latecomers on the scene of plant-thinking, to be involved with, to metamorphose, decay, and grow with that core. The shifting nature of the complex analogies between canonical figures, plant parts, and psychic faculties is but one example of vegetal movement featured in Hildegard's writings. Similarly, *viriditas* itself is not an entity, not a point of absolute repose meant to guarantee stability to the rest of the system, but energy on the move and at rest, greening and green, potential and fully actual. The efflorescence of Hildegard's activity in the most diverse fields—from medicine to music, from the invention of a language to the recording of visions—is also indicative of rooting in a generative and generous process, rather than doctrinaire insistence on a set of basic principles. She lets *viriditas* carry her thinking and doing (we all too eagerly transcribe this pair into theory and practice) wherever its winding paths might take them.

So, where are we? Where are these winding paths taking *us*? Listen for once to freshness: it will point the way.

AFTERWORD

Composer's Notes

WORKING ON, interpreting, or creating music with Hildegard of Bingen both poses demands and charts a path to freedom. My starting point in this attempt to interpret the contents of her music was the impossibility of re-creating something we might call an "authentic" or "stylistically correct" practice of hers after eight hundred years. The time that has elapsed between the origin and the execution in the present becomes decisive and dissolves all obligations for us to be credible interpreters. This holds, also, for the works of composers who are closer to us in time, such as Monteverdi, Bach, Mozart, and even those as close as the twentieth century, including Schönberg or Webern.

Hildegard of Bingen was not a composer in the sense we give the word today, a sense that probably does not extend further back than Beethoven. Hildegard was a general humanist and a seeker of science, who, I believe, sought God and harmony in and between all the chores she pursued and beings she cared for, whether texts, plants, stones, or something else. Perhaps, one can equate her way of working with that of Leonardo da Vinci. Her compositions or melodies, which are based on texts, really do not fit any of our musical categories today. We cannot distinguish her melodies from those by anonymous others. What we know is that there are songs, but we do not know whether they were performed a cappella or with some kind of instrumental accompaniment.

In this work of mine it became crucial to keep, in some way, Hildegard's voice as an extension of time, given that time is always a sort of extension. Real time does not exist but is always the past (it is always over). The voice as an instrument is also a changing part of the whole to take into account. Today, a voice may be just as much the voice of the instruments we have invented, the instruments that give our time a voice, as the voice of a person. For a form, I have followed Michael Marder's way of building separate sections with a modern flair, where solo predominates as a mass. Therefore, I have largely failed to make my Hildegard of Bingen music with a human voice, but have pursued the consequences of using our time, our instruments, and our techniques, where even electronics have their place. In my work, however, I have let Hildegard's material remain both understandable and hidden. I have used material reduced in terms of instruments, working to keep a constant low and meditative tone. In no way have I tried to interpret Hildegard's work, but have made my own music based on the enormous and important material she still gives to the world.

Peter Schuback
Täby, Sweden

ABBREVIATIONS

Acta

Acta sanctorum: Sanctae Hildegardis natales, res gestae, scripta, in Patriologia latina (PL), ed. J.-P. Migne (Paris, 1855), vol. 197, pp. 9–90

Analecta

Analecta sanctae Hildegardis, in Analecta sacra, vol. 8, ed. J.-B. Pitra (Monte Cassino, 1882)

Epist. (CCCM 91 [First Part] and CCCM 91A [Second Part])

Hildegardis Bingensis epistolarium, First Part, I–XC, ed. L. Van Acker, Corpus christianorum continuatio mediaevalis (CCCM), vol. 91 (Turnhout: Brepols, 1991); Second Part, XCI–CCLr, ed. L. Van Acker, CCCM, vol. 91A (Turnhout: Brepols, 1993)

ESSA (CCCM 226)

Explanatio symboli sancti Athanasii, ed. P. Evans, in Hildegardis Bingensis opera minora, CCCM, vol. 226 (Turnhout: Brepols, 2007), pp. 109–33

LDO (CCCM 92)

Hildegardis Bingensis Liber divinorum operum, ed. A. Derolez and P. Dronke, CCCM, vol. 92 (Turnhout: Brepols, 1996)

Ordo (CCCM 226)	*Ordo virtutum*, ed. P. Dronke, in *Hildegardis Bingensis opera minora*, CCCM, vol. 226 (Turnhout: Brepols, 2007), pp. 503–21
Physica (*PL* 197)	*Physica liber subtitilitatum diversarum naturarum creaturum*, in *Patrologia latina* (*PL*), ed. J.-P. Migne (Paris, 1855), vol. 197, pp. 1117–1352
PL	*Patrologiae cursus completus: Series latina* (*Patriologia latina*), ed. J.-P. Migne, 221 vols. (Paris, 1841–64)
Scivias	(CCCM 43) *Hildegardis Scivias*, ed. A. Führkötter, CCCM, vol. 43 (Turnhout: Brepols, 1978)
Symph.	*Symphonia armonie celestium revelationum*, ed. and trans. B. Newman, 2d ed. (Ithaca, NY: Cornell University Press, 1998)
TOQ (CCCM 226A)	*Triginta octo quaestionum solutiones*, ed. P. Evans, in *Hildegardis Bingensis opera minora II*, CCCM, vol. 226A (Turnhout: Brepols, 2016), pp. 111–28

Note: Some of Hildegard's works are also available in English translation. Among these, readers may wish to consult the following titles, arranged by year of publication:

Epistolarium	*The Letters of St. Hildegard of Bingen*, 3 vols., trans. Joseph L. Baird and Radd K. Ehrman (Oxford: Oxford University Press, 1994–2004)
Liber divinorum operum	*The Book of Divine Works*, trans. Nathaniel M. Campbell (Washington, DC: Catholic University of America Press, 2018)
Liber vitae meritorum	*The Book of the Rewards of Life*, trans. Bruce Hozeski (Oxford: Oxford University Press, 1994)

Physica	*Hildegard von Bingen's* Physica: *The Complete English Translation of Her Classic Work on Health and Healing,* trans. Priscilla Throop (Rochester, VT: Healing Arts Press, 1998)
Scivias	*Hildegard of Bingen: Scivias,* trans. Columbia Hart (Mahwah, NJ: Paulist Press, 1990)
Symphonia	*Symphonia: A Critical Edition of the "Symphonia Armonie Celestium Revelationum" (Symphony of the Harmony of Celestial Revelations),* ed. and trans. Barbara Newman, 2d ed. (Ithaca, NY: Cornell University Press, 1998)

INDEX

actuality, 14, 20, 26, 35, 44, 53, 63, 68–69, 81, 84, 127, 129, 151

Adam, 13–14, 45–46, 48–49, 96, 112–13, 138; name of, 34; rib of, 22–24, 112; voice of, 56–57, 60

agriculture, 48–49

allegory, 7, 17

angels, 56–57, 63, 69, 79; as messengers, 56, 81; voice of, 56–57, 60

angiosperms, 12

anima, 32–33, 41, 44, 50, 54, 62, 83, 144–45

animal, 7, 21, 36, 49–50, 54–55, 69, 105–6, 111–13, 119, 145, 150

ariditas, x, 7, 12, 14–15, 18, 27, 89–90, 100, 102–7, 113, 129

Aristotle, 32, 34, 47, 54, 61, 68, 95, 97, 123

articulation, 6, 55, 59, 62, 66, 135–36

atmosphere, 69, 78, 103, 106

Augustine, St., ix, 7, 26, 47, 63, 91, 97, 143–44

baptism, 7, 105

Bataille, Georges, 118

Beckett, Samuel, 106

becoming, 22, 43, 75, 93, 112; of becoming, 79; -world, 17, 79, 84

beginning, 12–14, 19, 40, 75–77, 79, 96, 113, 117–31, 142; absolute, 129; anarchic, 111, 117, 130–31; another, 19, 45, 120; without beginning, 120, 122–23, 126; of creation, 12–13, 16, 22, 118, 125–26; as head, 118; as middle, 22, 25, 77, 117; of middle, 75; new, 13–14, 107, 129

Bernard of Clairvaux, St., 73, 141–43

birth, 15, 25, 39, 41, 47–48, 50, 93, 105, 112–13, 141

body, 32, 34–35, 43–44, 53–56,

59, 67, 76, 82, 91, 103, 106–
7; love, 97, 112–13, 141–43;
mutable, 5; self-sacrifice of,
22

earth, 7–8, 11, 19, 21–22, 32–34,
49–50, 60, 78, 99–101, 103–
4, 112, 130; barren, 8, 12–13;
elemental, 32; as origin of
plants and humans, 33–34;
return to, 15, 49, 106, 121; and
sky, 22, 50, 140–43
Eberhard of Bamberg, Bishop, 79
Eckhart, Meister, 91
ecology, 3–7, 55, 57, 84, 102, 111,
131, 143, 146, 150–51; of kissing, 136–37, 143; and soul, 55;
symphonic, 57; theological,
3–7, 12, 89, 92–93, 136–37,
146, 150–51
edification, 137, 142–44, 146
eidetic, 37
elements, the, 32, 46, 57, 69, 99,
103, 105, 110, 113, 131, 139–40
embrace, 92, 97, 119, 128, 135,
142–46; cosmic, 97; edifying,
137, 139–40, 145–46; of the
heart, 79
Empedocles, 32
end, 13–14, 16, 22, 25–27, 40, 43,
45, 81, 107, 117–24, 127–29;
and beginning, 4, 14, 19, 63,
68, 75–77, 79, 111, 117–24,
127–29, 131, 142; fructified,
22; suspended, 16, 111, 125,
128; of the world, 6, 8, 28, 128
energy, 13–14, 17–19, 25, 97, 99,
119, 124, 151; divine, 18, 37,
102, 124, 129–31; false, 13,

106–7; growing, 25, 27; production, 106
enlightenment, 108
entropy, 13, 25, 90, 103
eschaton, 77
essence 16–17, 27, 35, 47, 78, 108,
124
eternity, 7, 11, 16, 21, 39, 73, 77,
80–81, 111, 117–18, 128, 146
Eugenius, Pope, 77, 79
Eve, 13–14, 22, 24, 46, 112–13, 138
exegesis, 26, 39–41, 67, 142, 149
existence, 4, 6, 12–14, 16–17, 20,
25–26, 31, 33–36, 45, 54–56,
63, 77, 81, 84, 89, 96, 99, 102,
111, 120–26, 129–31; collaborative, 17, 54, 58, 67; divine,
47, 124–25; finite, 4, 14, 25,
33, 106–7, 130, 150; human, 17,
82; sabbatical, 48–49
exposure, 15, 64, 92, 99, 139–40,
145

faith, 26, 40, 44, 90, 144–46
Fall, the, 12–15, 20, 23, 25, 40, 47,
49, 56–57, 60, 65, 92, 113
fecundity, 22, 24, 95–96, 126, 130
femininity, 20, 37, 76, 98
fermentation, 43–45
field, 7, 38–39, 47
finis, 123, 128
finitude, 97, 107, 127–30, 150
fire, 4, 32, 43, 83–85, 89–114;
dark, 91–92, 114; eternal, 107;
of God, 83–84, 90, 96–97;
metaphysics of, 113; oppositional, 103, 106–9; as plant,
95–97, 99–102; powers of,
21, 92–94, 98–99, 107–8,

110, 139–40; of justice, 91;
rootedness in, 21, 25, 93, 99
surface, 15–17, 19, 25, 46–47, 84,
92, 131, 135, 138–41, 143–45;
aesthetic, 16, 46–47; and
depth, 27, 144–45; ontological, 46; vegetal, 15–16, 139
symbol, symbolism, 7, 17, 21, 34,
120
symphony, symphonicity, 5, 53–67,
127; green, 11, 53; of being, 5,
54, 58, 67; of justice, 62–63,
65–66; of soul, 54–56, 61,
64–66
synecdoche, 5
synesthesia, 53, 57, 64, 110, 123
system, 4, 13, 33, 42, 62, 119, 151

tears, 64–65
teleology, 15, 24, 43
terminus, 128
Tertullian, 39
theandric, the, 73, 76, 110, 141
theography, 36
theology, 3–7, 12, 33, 36–37, 39–
41, 45, 47–49, 54, 60, 76, 89,
91–93, 124, 136–37, 143, 146,
149–51; apophatic, 91; negative, 117, 122; vegetalized, 5,
37, 41, 105, 151
thinking, 8, 36, 149–51; plant-, 36,
119, 150–51; and singing, 5, 18
tikkun olam, 60
time, 15, 17, 19, 26, 44, 46, 49,
62–63, 67, 75–79, 81–83, 111,
113, 118, 121, 125, 130–31,
138, 149; appointed, 15, 75–
76; backflow of, 15, 76, 78,
93; circular, 121, 130; of the
middle, 77, 81, 143; planetary,
121; seasonal, 76, 93, 121;

secular, 14; stretching of,
62–63
to threptikon, 47, 61
touch, 7, 18, 28, 48, 50, 53, 123,
136–40, 142–46
transcendence, 40
tree, 11, 35–43, 48–50, 78, 80,
106–8, 110–12, 131–32; of
cross, 14, 48, 110–11; of
Jesse, 40; of Knowledge of
Good and Evil, 14, 20, 24,
46, 138; sap, 34, 39–42; soul
as, 36, 42, 50, 54, 97–98;
verticality of, 40; world-,
35–36
Trinitarian theology, 75, 98–99,
118, 126

unconscious, the, 21, 41, 67
universal, universality, 33–34,
39–40, 60–61, 101–2, 142;
exception, 22, 101; greenness,
12, 34; justice, 60; root, 37,
40, 99

vegetality, 11, 20–21, 28, 46–47,
95, 105, 111–13
vibration, 5, 19, 53–54, 57–59, 64,
66, 68, 130, 140
Virgil, 13
virginity, 20–21, 25–26, 38, 75–76,
81, 95, 107–8
virility, 19–21, 28, 38, 76
vitality, 4, 6–7, 11, 17, 35, 47, 54,
56, 61, 80, 82, 122–23, 145, 150
voice, 11, 17–19, 28, 54–60, 66–
69, 127–28; angelic, 56–57, 60,
69; as body, 54–56, 58–59, 68–
69, 145; living, 55–56, 67–69;
middle, 77, 81; reverberating,
6, 54–55, 57, 127

weeds, 48

weight, 4, 21, 145

wheat, 32, 43–44

William of Conches, 13

winter, 13–14, 17, 42

wisdom, 3, 35–36, 42–46, 54, 137–39; and fruit, 35, 44–46; and maturity, 36, 42–43; of love, 137, 139

womb, 33, 73–75, 77–78, 92, 95

word, 56, 73–79, 120–21, 125–29, 131, 135–41; anarchy of, 126–27; divine, 17–19, 73–76, 79, 120–21, 125–27, 129, 131, 137, 141, 151; incarnation of, 75–76, 79, 136; mystical, 135–36, 139–41; sending of, 76–78; spoken, 6, 74, 135, 138

world, 5–6, 8, 11, 16–18, 22, 32, 34–36, 44, 50, 57–60, 62–63, 65–69, 74, 76–77, 79, 82, 84, 90–93, 97–98, 103–4, 111, 118, 126, 128–31, 136, 138–41, 143, 145–46, 150; becoming-, 17, 79, 84; chords of, 58, 65–66; -creation, 69, 93, 124, 136, 150; destruction, 6, 8, 18, 90, 103, 106–7; fallen, 42, 74, 84, 92; greening of, 17, 20, 123–24, 150; history, 14; infinite, 128, 146; of plants, 14, 20, 22, 59, 77, 98, 150; shipwrecked, 65

Printed in the USA
CPSIA information can be obtained
at www.ICGtesting.com
LVHW051204230124
769723LV00026B/398